Reminiscences of Early Free Methodism

By
Rev. Edward Payson Hart

Senior General Superintendent Of the Free
Methodist Church of North America

With
An Introduction
By
Rev. Burton R. Jones

First Fruits Press
Wilmore, Kentucky
c2016

Reminiscences of early Free Methodism.
By Rev. Edward Payson Hart, Senior General Superintendent of the Free Methodist Church of
North America.

First Fruits Press, ©2016
Previously published by the Free Methodist Publishing House, 1913.

ISBN: 9781621715740 (print), 9781621715757 (digital), 9781621715764 (kindle)

Digital version at http://place.asburyseminary.edu/freemethodistbooks/24/

For all other uses, contact:

First Fruits Press
B.L. Fisher Library
Asbury Theological Seminary
204 N. Lexington Ave.
Wilmore, KY 40390
http://place.asburyseminary.edu/firstfruits

Hart, Edward Payson.
    Reminiscences of early Free Methodism / by Edward Payson Hart ; with an introduction by
Burton R. Jones. -- Wilmore, Kentucky : First Fruits Press, ©2016.
        xxi, 259 pages, [1] leaf of plates : portrait ; 21 cm.
        Reprint. Previously published: Chicago, Illinois : Free Methodist Publishing House,
        1913.
        ISBN - 13: 9781621715740 (pbk.)
        1. Free Methodist Church of North America--History. I. Title.
BX8413.H3 2016   287.97

Cover design by Jon Ramsay

asburyseminary.edu
800.2ASBURY
204 North Lexington Avenue
Wilmore, Kentucky 40390

First Fruits
THE ACADEMIC OPEN PRESS OF ASBURY SEMINARY

First Fruits Press
The Academic Open Press of Asbury Theological Seminary
204 N. Lexington Ave., Wilmore, KY 40390
859-858-2236
first.fruits@asburyseminary.edu
asbury.to/firstfruits

Yours in Jesus
Edward S. Hart

REMINISCENCES

OF

EARLY FREE METHODISM

...BY...

REV. EDWARD PAYSON HART

Senior General Superintendent
Of the Free Methodist Church of North America

WITH

AN INTRODUCTION

BY

REV. BURTON R. JONES

CHICAGO, ILLINOIS.
FREE METHODIST PUBLISHING HOUSE
1132 WASHINGTON BOULEVARD
1913

PREFACE.

AT THE earnest request of the editor of the *Free Methodist* much of the matter contained in the following pages was originally prepared for publication in that paper. The writer had no thought that the articles would ever appear in book form. But as many of the readers of the sketches, as they appeared in the *Free Methodist*, have expressed a desire to have them in a more convenient and durable form I have by advice of our publishing agents consented to their publication, and have revised the matter as it originally appeared, adding several entirely new chapters. As to literary merit these pages are not open to criticism since no claim in that direction is made.

Another volume giving a more general account of the work East and West is contemplated.

Alameda, Cal.   E. P. HART.

CONTENTS.

PAGE.

CHAPTER I.: Origin of Free Methodist Church—B. T. Roberts, L. Stiles, J. McCreery and Others Expelled from Genesee Conference of Methodist Episcopal Church—Roberts' Appeal Denied by General Conference—Preaching of J. W. Redfield Important Factor in Formation of Church—Doctor Redfield Labors at Saint Charles, Illinois—The Way Opened for the Doctor's Work at Marengo, Illinois, by a Dream—Some at Marengo Who Knew God—A Mother's Protracted Meeting—Joseph G. Terrill Converted—Doctor Redfield Labors at Elgin, Illinois—J. G. Terrill Receives Increased Light—Tribute to Joseph G. Terrill—C. E. Harroun Saved, Becomes a Strong Preacher.   1-9

CHAPTER II.: Doctor Redfield Begins Meeting at Marengo—Young Lawyer Invited to the First Service—Fear that the Doctor May Fail Through Embarrassment—Fear Dispelled and a Young Convert Dazzled by Light—Doctor's Manner, Preaching and Prayers—Odd Character Startles Congregation—Many Rush to the Altar—Young Methodist Girl Gets Fully Saved—Alone with the Doctor—Rather Searching Questions—Young Converts Discouraged —Tide Soon Turns—Sweeping Revival—Need of a Fog-Splitter—Village Drayman Saved—Lawyer's Wife Gets Salvation   10-18

CHAPTER III.: Doctor Redfield Preaches at Woodstock—Brings the Pastor to the Point—I. H. Fairchilds—Work Opposed at Saint Charles—Transition of Methodist Episcopal Church—Pastor Howard, of Methodist Episcopal Church, Reads Out Members Without Trial—Doctor Redfield Denied Methodist Episcopal Pulpit—Universalist Church is Secured — Rally of Holiness People — Benjamin Hackney—Great Sermon—Persecuted Saints Rent Hall and Send for Joseph Terrill—Meeting at Clintonville—Work at Vermont Street, etc., Increases in Power—Work at Franklinville Church—Presiding Elder Warns the People—Preacher in Charge Changes Front—People Petition for Change of Preachers—Both Senior and Junior Preachers Returned—Father Bishop Opens His House for Holiness Meeting—Preacher in Charge Tries to Get Control of Meeting—The Best Family—Meetings Opened in Brick Schoolhouse—Large Methodist Episcopal Class Formed—Father Bishop's Family Attend—They are Cited for Trial—Unjustly Condemned—Expelled—Preacher in Close Place—Form Earnest Christian Band—Forty Days' Fast..   19–27

CHAPTER IV.: Writer Feels His Need of Salvation—Infidel Lawyer Settles the Question—An Earnest Seeker—Makes Preparations to Attend School of the Prophets — Plans Thwarted—One of God's Doctors of Divinity—Seeking the Experience of Entire Sanctification—Trying Tests—Way Opens to Preach—Secretary of Lodge—Intellectual Culture Desirable — Licensed to Preach — Receives Works of Edward Payson—The Converted Blacksmith—No Lack of Confidence—He is Killed in Battle Before Richmond—Hooper Crews—Appointment as Junior Preacher on Lynnville Circuit—Brother Campbell Preacher in Charge—Meetings in Kendrick Schoolhouse—Aunt Polly Kendrick—Demonstrations Annoy Preacher in Charge—Grove Meeting at Lynnville—Send for Seymour Coleman

—First Meeting with Joseph Travis—Storm Stayed
by Prayer—Hotel Keeper's Wife Angry........... 28-39

CHAPTER V.: Rev. Travis Stops at Lynnville—Visits
Methodist Episcopal Camp-Meeting in Wisconsin
—A Runaway—Reach Camp-Ground—Meet Brother
Fox—Introduced to Presiding Elder—Looked Upon
with Some Degree of Suspicion—Preach but Once
—Start for Saint Charles, Illinois, Camp-Meeting—
Stop at Marengo, Illinois—A Tempting Offer
Rejected—Reach Saint Charles Camp-Ground
Early Friday Morning—Introduced Brother Travis
to Doctor Redfield—First Meeting with Rev. B. T.
Roberts—Power of God Present at Meeting—Some
Degree of Wildness—Seymour Coleman Explains
Extravagances—Bishop Girl Sings "Gideon"—Mar-
ried to Bishop Girl—Brother Travis Joins the New
Church—Is Sent to Saint Louis—Take Wife to
Circuit — Good Sister Thinks Bride is Rather
Plainly Attired—Good Service on Sabbath—Visit
Lynnville Appointment — Hotel Keeper's Wife
Pleads for Universalists—Return to Marengo at
Close of Conference Year—Notify Presiding Elder
to Drop Name from Conference—No Appointment
Ready in New Church—Decide to Step into First
Open Door 40-49

CHAPTER VI.: Political Excitement of Fall of 1860—
Door Unexpectedly Opens to Preach at Belvidere,
Illinois—David Cooper and John Horan—Appointment in Universalist Church at Belvidere—Lucius
Matlack Yields Pulpit—Doctor Redfield Preaches
Sabbath Evening to Large Congregation—Accompany the Doctor and Wife to Ogle County—Brother
Terrill had Raised up a Work There—J. W. Dake
and Others Enter the Work—Doctor Redfield Goes
on to Aurora, Illinois—Is Stricken Down with Paralysis—Secure Congregationalist Church at Belvidere—Large Congregations—Form Class and Pur-

chase Church Property—Discipline Adopted at
Clintonville—James Mathews Takes the Work at
Belvidere—Go to Marengo—Commence Meetings
in Street—Finally Secure Metropolitan Hall—Judah
Mead Holds Quarterly Meeting—A Loud Time—
Open Doors of Church—Three Join—Village Drayman Joins Later—Buy Lot—Move Back Old House
and Make a Church of it—Build Permanent House
of Worship in the Spring—Fearful Tornado—Conference Appoints to Saint Charles, etc........... 50–57

CHAPTER VII.: Incidents of Work at Belvidere and
Marengo—Discipline Forbids Secrecy—Convinced
that Oath-Bound Secret Orders are Wrong—Getting
Out of the Lodge............................... 58–64

CHAPTER VIII.: Pleasant Year at Saint Charles—Meet-
ings in Old Court House at Geneva—German Man
and Wife Saved from Catholicism—Child Sick but
Get Encouragement—Saloon Keeper Convicted—
Set About Building Church—Plans Enlarged—Prop-
erty Sold—Onslaught of Roughs at Saint Charles
Camp-Meeting—Newell Day Injured—Ordained
Deacon at Clintonville Fall of 1860—Requested to
go to Michigan—Sent to Marengo with Understand-
ing I am to Visit Michigan—Return to Marengo—
Rev. J. W. Redfield Dies—Brother Roberts Attends
Funeral at Marengo—Impressive Scene at Funeral
—Doctor Redfield's Testimony—Steps Over into
Heaven—Illinois Conference Assumes Respectable
Proportions—Cyrus Underwood—J. W. Dake Raises
up Work in Bureau County—Joseph Travis—N. D.
Fanning—Thomas LaDue—M. V. Clute.......... 65–79

CHAPTER IX.: C. E. Harroun's Reason for not Going
to Church to Preach—Great Storm—Arrange to
Visit Michigan—Failed in Getting Rates from Chicago, but Got an Incident—Picture of Imagination
not Realized—Gloomy Outlook—Wife Keeps up
Courage—Find House of Father Jones—A Hearty

Welcome—Attend Methodist Episcopal Conformist
Church—How the Way was Opened for Free Meth-
odism in Michigan—Meeting at Milan well Attended
—Favorable Impression of Free Methodist Church
—Sister Lewis Lays Aside Bonnet Trimmed with
Artificials, Puts on Veil and Comes to the Com-
munion—Hold Meetings in Father Jones' Neigh-
borhood—Happy Jimmy 80-90

CHAPTER X.: Visit Otter Creek—Cold Reception—Stop
at Rum Tavern—Visit from House to House—Find
People Nearly all Lutherans or Catholics—Have
Family Prayers with Landlord and Wife—Wife an
Old Once-in-grace-always-in-grace Backslider—
Return to Ida Station—"If Man Living Here Should
Get Saved it would Stir this whole Country"—Get-
ting Homesick—Determined to Make or Break—
Commence in Plues Schoolhouse—Decide to Hold
Afternoon Meetings in Private Houses—House of
John Plues Open—Away to Attend Funeral—Sister
Hart Leads Meeting at House of Plues—Encounters
Sneering Scoffer—Scoffer Cornered and Begins to
Break—John Plues—Mrs. Plues Gets Blessed—
Forbid to Read Bible and Pray — "Samantha,
do You Think Those Preachers would Come and
Pray for Me?"—Sister Plues Calls at Timothy G.'s
for Preachers—"Timothy, John wants you to come,
too"—Choker for Timothy—Preacher Caught up—
"Am I in the Straight Way?"—Praying for Neigh-
bors—Start Out to Pray with Neighbors—Nearly
all the Neighbors Break and Get Saved—Plues
Opens His House to Entertain Preachers—Laborers
Raised up—Elsworth Leonardson—Confessing a
Call to Preach—Soon at it—Meeting Classes—Plan
to go Home—"You have Got Us into this Boat and
You must see Us Through"—"By the Grace of God
We will"—Return to Illinois—Meet with Opposition
in Going Back to Michigan—Brother Roberts Sanc-

tions Our Return—C. S. Gitchell Takes Work at
Marengo 91-106

CHAPTER XI.: Stop at Mishawaka, Indiana—Go on to
Osseo—Disappointed in Appointment—Baby Sick
—A Dilemma—Lord Opens the Way—Methodist
Pastor Greets Us—An Old Friend—Baby Better—
A Fruitful Valentine—Little Heathen Shown—Mrs.
Frink Breaks Down and Gets Saved—Grove-Meet-
ing in Plues Neighborhood—Party from Hillsdale
County—Brother Roberts Does not Arrive—Put up
a Man to Preach—People Take Him for Our Bishop
—Are Disappointed—Go to Plues' Ball-room to Get
Ready to Preach—"Glory to God, Brother Hart,
Roberts Has Come!"—Hasten to Grove—Brother
Roberts Refuses to Preach—But Exhorts—Hills-
dale Party Anxious to Join—Go to Saint Charles
Camp-meeting—On Return Stop at Hillsdale—
Refuse to Organize Class—Return to Plues Neigh-
borhood—Urged to Visit Hillsdale—Cannot, for
Want of Means—Money Provided—Decide to Go—
Sister Coon Meets Us at Hillsdale—Meeting at
Steamburg—John Ellison and Wife Get Light.....107-121

CHAPTER XII.: Brother Ellison Attends Sabbath Afternoon Appointment—He Attends Grove-Meeting at
Ida—Gets Fully Saved—Attend Illinois Conference
at Saint Charles—Memorial Services for J. W. Redfield and Ira G. Gould—Report of Committee on
State of the Work—Return to Ida—W. D. Bishop
and Wife go to Michigan—"Lord Jesus, Drive Back
Powers of Hell!"—Revival Breaks Out—Hold on
for Four Weeks—Signs and Wonders............122-132

CHAPTER XIII.: Open Work on Huron River—Hunter
Convicted—Uncle Horace Ash—Jim's Team on the
Altar—Uncle Johnny Clark Saved—One of His
Later Testimonies—John Ellison Preaches Holiness
—Becomes Unpopular—Dismissed from Pastorate
—Some of His Members Stand by Him—Called to

Organize Class Where Brother Ellison Preaches—
"Go Ahead, Brother Hart, I'll go the Whole Hog"—
Good Advice Received—Work Spreads into Branch
County—Sylvester Forbes—Selling Soul for Pail of
Sap—Thou Art the Man—Scruples About Baptism
Removed—Powerful Camp-Meetings—On the "Old
Line"...133-142

CHAPTER XIV.: Attend Bergen, New York, Camp-
Meeting—Loren Stiles—Fay Purdy—Blind Henry—
Joseph McCreery—Try to Preach—Introduced to
McCreery—Was that You "Hollerin' so Out There?"
—Joseph and Benjamin—"A Living Christ"—Meet-
ing at White Church—Spirit of Dead Indian—
Preach on Spiritualism—Great Break—Sister Hart
Dreams of Serpent—Medium's Daughter Saved—
Return to Illinois—Help in Meeting at Aurora—
"Girl, All Doing Well"—Fail to Catch the Train—
Short of Funds—Lack made up—Attend Illinois
Conference at Marengo—Go to Morenci, Michigan,
to Open Work—Brothers Osgood and Goss—Get
Appointment in Campbellite Swamp—Come Out
Ahead—Conclude to Remove to Monroe County—
Snow-Bound.....................................143-159

CHAPTER XV.: Michigan Conference Organized—
Lively Camp-Meeting—County Papers have a con-
troversy — Work Advertised — Short Conference
Year—First Free Methodist Church in Michigan
Built—Joseph Travis Presides at Session of Confer-
ence—Dedicates Church—Preacher's Necessities
Met—Gray Family—Elected with John Plues to
General Conference—Police Come in—C. H, Love-
joy Admitted on His Picture—J. McCreery Admit-
ted on His Face—J. McCreery Delegate to General
Conference — Log Rolling — Last Characteristic
Speech of Joseph McCreery 160-167

CHAPTER XVI.: Work at Windsor, Ohio—Quite a Scene
at Christmas Eve Service—Going Through with

Flying Colors—Family Separated—"Lord Only Knows Whether We'll All get Together Again"—Hold Meeting at Coldwater, Michigan—Spiritualists and Mormons Try to Ring in—Seeing Devils—Start for Marengo, Illinois—Train too Slow—Edson A. Kimball—Cyrus Underwood Holds Meeting at Elgin, Illinois—Change Work with Brother Underwood—Stumbling Stone Johnson—Attend Michigan Conference at Coldwater—Illinois Conference Held at Elgin—President of Wheaton College Visits Conference...168-178

CHAPTER XVII.: Work Spreads in Illinois Conference —D. P. Reed—Brother and Sister Dudman—Lewis Bailey—Third Session Michigan Conference—"W. D. Bishop and One to be Supplied"—Conference Session af White Church—B. R. Jones Joins on Trial—Is Ordained—Elected Chairman—Editor —General Superintendent—Work Opens at Cooperville, Michigan—W. R. Cusick—Hold Meeting in Congregational Church—Revival Breaks Out—Leading Ladies in Town Earnestly Seeking—Uncle Tom and Aunt Rhoda Watson—Lord Breaks Down Opposition to Work—Work Prospers at Coopersville—New Church Built—Spreads East—Hold Quarterly Meeting in Log Schoolhouse, Fifteen Minutes Intermission Between the Logs...........179-187

CHAPTER XVIII.: Grove-Meeting at Berlin, Michigan —North Woods Full of Them—In Fall 1870 Conference Held at Holland, Ohio—Appointed to Toledo District—John Ellison Appointed to Grand Rapids District—Meeting Near Concord, Michigan—Meetings at Eckford—A. V. Leonardson Appointed to Concord and Eckford—Attention Called to Old School Property at Spring Arbor—Session of Conference Appointed to Concord Work but Held at Spring Arbor—Fears About Entertainment—Conference Well Cared for—Brother Roberts Meets

Old College Chum—Committee Appointed to Locate
School—Conference at Delta, Ohio—Work There—
Dedicate Church at Delta—Meetings in Toledo,
Ohio—Work Opens in Madison, Michigan—Lafay-
ette Reed 188-198

CHAPTER XIX.: Conference at Delta, Ohio—Spring
Arbor School—Laid by for a Rest—Providentially
Cared for—Life Despaired of—Lord Undertakes—
Striking Vision—Location of School Decided on—
Teachers Secured — Tramp Rescued — Becomes
Tutor to Our Future Principal—The First Faculty—
California Boys Helped—Our Schools a Blessing...199-212

CHAPTER XX.: Start Out on District Work—Meeting
at Jackson, Michigan—A Prophecy Fulfilled—
Conference Session at Coopersville—Remarkable
Sermon—General Conferences—J. Mackey Takes
Free Methodist—General Conference at Albion,
New York—Elected General Superintendent......213-221

CHAPTER XXI.: Attend Meetings in Pennsylvania—
Clifford Barrett—Franklin, Pennsylvania, Camp-
Meeting—J. B. Corey—Boys in the Pit—Way Opens
to Summerfield, Ohio—Visit Attica, Lawrenceburg,
Indiana, etc.—Cincinnati, Ohio—Turning the Hose
on Them—Go on to Summerfield—Receive Hearty
Welcome—Church Already Built—J. M. Rounds—
Dr. Taylor....................................222-230

CHAPTER XXII.: The New Preacher and Wife—Large
Congregations — Truth Takes Hold — Sorry Hart
Came—Decide to Bring Matters to a Focus—
Brought to a Decision—Earnest Seekers—Inappro-
priate Singing—Meetings from 11 a. m. to 11 p. m.
—Slain of the Lord are Many—Footprints of J. B.
Finley—Billy Barnes—Jennie H.—Demonstrations
Nothing New—Blacksmith Converted—He Gets
Light on Entire Holiness—Open Church Doors—
Meetings at Freedom, East Union, etc.—Frail
Woman Makes a Stir—Old Local Preacher—

Classes Organized in Noble County—W. H. James Given Charge—Preaches at Perryopolis—J. W. Headly and Wife—Church Door Locked—"Let Them Go"—Sister Headly Joins—Brother Headly Joins on Probation—Licensed—Becomes District Elder...231-242

CHAPTER XXIII.: First Experience in Presiding at Eastern Conferences — Asa Abell — "Don't Sing That"—Responsibility Felt—John Reddy—At the Centennial Exposition — Camp-meeting at Salamanca, N. Y.—R. W. Hawkins—Standing for the Old Landmarks—Spirit Poured Out at Reading of Hymn—West Randolph, N. Y.—Meetings in Baptist Church—Stir Among Infidels and Baptists— Miss Ella Hapgood—Young Convert Wins a Universalist Family.................................243-249

CHAPTER XXIV.: At Oberlin, O.—Crowded Hall—College Chapel and Finney's Church—Finney's Theology—Devoted and Meek Saints—Burlington, Iowa —M. L. Vorhies comes on—A Tramp Preacher— Brother Vorheis' Railroad Song—German Catholic Old Lady—John Burg—Church Built on North Hill —General Conference of 1882 Held here—San Jose California—Vacant Store Rented—Street Meetings With Ross Taylor — Interested Englishman—He Wishes to Join—"Nothing will Trouble me but the Smoke"—Brother Brown's Will — Growth of the Church Remarkable—Many Men and Women of Noble Character.................................250-259

INTRODUCTORY NOTE.

AT different periods in the history of the church crises have arisen at which it became necessary for God to thrust out extraordinary men, "endued with power from on high," to change existing moral conditions. These men, sent of God, have gone forth as the voice of one crying in the wilderness, "Prepare ye the way of the Lord, make his paths straight."

The Free Methodist movement was born of a divine purpose. After the natural conservator of Methodism had lapsed into formality and worldliness God placed his seal of authority upon a few holy men and sent them forth to awaken the slumbering energies of the church and the world and exemplify a type of piety at once deep, wholesome and consistent. Evidently this movement was of God and its leaders divinely commissioned. Yet its right to an existence has been repeatedly challenged, and it has been cast into a furnace of criticism heated seven times hotter than for any other church of the last half century, but it has thus far escaped even the smell of fire on its sacred garments. The result of these testings has been, and should ever be, to keep its adherents humble before God and inspire them to pursue with even greater intensity the course outlined at the beginning.

The mission of this book is to call the attention of its readers to the important lessons taught by the past history of the church, to note the warnings that it conveys for the future, and thus safely fortify against the perils that threaten the life of the church. History affords examples of churches which have "triumphed over adversity but could not bear the test of success."

The encouraging results already attained should inspire the church with a firmer faith in God and in the means employed for the promotion of his work, and with a spirit of self-sacrificing devotion to those Bible principles so closely related to our denominational existence.

But the church cannot live on past history. "The mill will never grind with the water that has passed." There must be aggression along legitimate lines. "To maintain the Bible standard of religion," to seek the salvation of all classes and to spread scriptural holiness has ever been, and should ever be, the mission of the Free Methodist church.

To the many in and out of the church who will read these reminiscences the author needs no introduction. And with many of these a personal acquaintance with him and knowledge of his ministry of over forty years will insure to the book a hearty greeting.

The author of this volume writes from personal experience and observation in the ministry of the Free Methodist church. Having been closely related to the Free Methodist movement from its beginning, few men living are as competent as he is to throw light on the practical events connected with the rise and progress of the church. He has not attempted to discuss opinions and methods, but simply to relate facts and narrate events. His extreme modesty would not admit of his saying much of himself or of his relation to the revivals he reports. He has entered no further into the relation of the events of his own life than seemed necessary to give an intelligent account of the religious movement with which he stands so closely related.

In early manhood Mr. Hart made choice of the law as a profession, to the study of which he applied himself for a short period. Soon after his conversion he received a divine call to the ministry of the gospel. He responded to the call, and thus his gifts and capabilities were preserved for the upbuilding of the Redeemer's kingdom. With the divine commission written in living letters of light over the entrance of his lifework, he bade a final adieu to

every worldly ambition and identified himself with a
movement under conditions which enabled him to
assist in building from the foundation up an organization which was fully committed to the mainte-
nance of the fundamental principle of Methodism.

Of his extraordinary ability to adapt the truth of
God to the necessities of mankind, of his earnestness
and eloquence, I need make no mention. He is
well known throughout the church as an efficient
evangelist and an able minister of the gospel of
Christ. The redemption of mankind and the building up of the church in righteousness and true holiness has ever been the master passion of his heart.
Ably assisted by his devoted, consecrated wife, he
has led the hosts of the Lord from conquering to
conquest, brought heavenly balm to many a sorrow-
ing heart, and been instrumental in turning many to
righteousness who will one day shine among the
stars in the celestial firmament.

This brief outline, covering a space of about
twenty-two years, bears upon its face the marks of a
thorough knowledge of the origin and mission of the
Free Methodist church. The doctrines preached
and the measures employed could but insure the
purity and permanence of the work wrought. The
author has endeavored to fix the attention of the
reader upon the various influences which have aided

in moulding our denominational character and producing our distinctive features.

The careful study of this book is important to the proper development of the church. How can the younger members of the church fully appreciate what they enjoy unless they know how it came to be?

The present generation of the church should be armed with those qualities that make for spiritual success.

This volume will prove valuable to all who are interested in the higher spiritual development of the church at large. It is offered with the sincere hope that its readers may profit by the lessons which the past history of the church teaches, and place a higher value upon the precious heritage of gospel liberty which is handed down to us in trust for the generations which are to follow.

BURTON R. JONES.

Jackson, Michigan, April, 1903.

REMINISCENCES OF
EARLY FREE METHODISM.

CHAPTER I.

"There are moments in life that are never forgot,
　Which brighten and brighten as time steals away;
Oh! these hallowed remembrances cannot decay,
　But they come on the soul with a magical thrill,
And in days that are darkest they kindly will stay,
　And the heart in its last throbs will beat with them still."

"THE Free Methodist church had its origin in necessity and not in choice." Its existence is not due to the efforts of ambitious men who sought notoriety by founding a new sect, but rather to the self-denying labors of those who took care of the conscience and left results with God." What are usually referred to as "our issues" are incidental rather than fundamental.

The men providentially raised up as the founders of this movement stood solidly upon the platform of scriptural holiness and were jealous only for moral purity. But the righteousness for which they contended was the same in character as that ascribed to

the Son of God: "Thou hast loved righteousness
and hated iniquity; therefore God, even thy God,
hath anointed thee with the oil of gladness above thy
fellows" (Heb. 1:9). The holiness they demanded
was not that sickly sentimentalism which, baptized
in the name of Christianity, is loud in its protesta-
tions of love for righteousness but dares not strike
one effectual blow at iniquity. These bold reformers,
in their hatred of and uncompromising opposition
to iniquity, soon came to questions involving moral
issues, and they were not slow in taking their stand
or unequivocal in defending their position.

Early in the fifties Rev's. B. T. Roberts, Loren
Stiles, Joseph McCreery and other members of the
Genesee conference of the Methodist Episcopal
church saw, as they believed, evidences of a growing
departure from scriptural Christianity and original
Methodism. At the session of the conference held
at Le Roy in the fall of 1857 Rev. B. T. Roberts was
tried and declared guilty of immoral conduct for
writing, and publishing in the *Northern Independent*,
an article entitled "New School Methodism." Repri-
manded by the bishop he went to his new charge at
Pekin with increased determination to be true to
God. During the following year George W. Estes of
Brockport, New York, in connection with the article
"New School Methodism," published in pamphlet

form an account of the trial of B. T. Roberts. At the next session of the conference, held at Perry, New York, Rev. Roberts, under a charge of "contumacy," was brought to trial for republishing and circulating the article on "New School Methodism;" and, although Mr. Estes on the witness stand testified that he was entirely responsible for the publication of the pamphlet, Rev. Roberts was declared guilty of immoral conduct and expelled from the conference and church. The expulsion of Stiles and others on trivial charges soon followed.

Brother Roberts took an appeal to the ensuing general conference which met in the spring of 1860, at Buffalo, New York. The appeal was not entertained. All hope of redress being cut off, these men of God knew of no way but to organize a new church, which organization was effected at a convention held at Pekin, New York, August 23, 1860.

Rev. Doctor Redfield, a homeopathic physician and a licensed local preacher of the Methodist Episcopal church, had been largely instrumental in promoting the work of holiness in western New York. He was a man of a very sensitive, retiring nature, but in his pulpit ministrations, under the baptism of the Spirit, his appeals and flights of eloquence at times were almost unearthly. The awakening on the subject of scriptural holiness, which invariably characterized the labors of Doctor Redfield, resulted in the formation of the Free Methodist church.

In June, 1856, we find Doctor Redfield, by invitation of the pastor, Rev. David Sherman, engaged in a revival meeting in the Methodist Episcopal church at St. Charles, Illinois. Rev. Sherman had known the doctor in New England, and, having taken a transfer to the Rock River conference, and being desirous of promoting the work of holiness on his charge, had written Doctor Redfield requesting him to come and assist him in a series of revival services. Father and Mother Foot, Brother and Sister Osborne and many others of the members of the society fell in with the doctor's preaching and methods, and a remarkable work of saving grace followed. A large number entered into the experience of entire sanctification, and many were converted.

The doctor labored in the west at different points for two or three years. In January, 1858, Rev. Vance, pastor of the Methodist Episcopal church at Marengo, Illinois, where I then lived, commenced a protracted meeting which, in a few weeks, resulted in some sixty accessions to the church. The pastor's health failed, and the members, feeling that the meeting ought to be continued, were anxious to find some one to take the lead and carry on the work.

My father, who was a class-leader, dreamed one

night that he saw Doctor Redfield walking up the aisle of the church. Father had never met the doctor, but had heard my mother, who had met him some years before in Vermont, frequently speak of him as a remarkable revivalist. Father laughingly spoke to some of the members about his dream, when a Sister Barron exclaimed, "Why, Doctor Redfield! there is a revivalist by that name who has held meetings at St. Charles." A letter was at once sent to St. Charles inquiring as to the whereabouts of the doctor, and reply was received that he was engaged in a meeting at Elgin. As my mother was acquainted with the doctor and his wife, she was delegated to go to Elgin and invite them to come to Marengo. As I was a young convert I accompanied mother. The doctor said he would go, provided the pastor and official board would give him full control and allow him to conduct the meeting in his own way. When we reported, the pastor objected very strongly to this proviso; but the members finally prevailed on him to allow the doctor to have full control.

During the weeks preceding, in the protracted effort, the members had been getting down before the Lord, and so were in good condition to receive the plain, searching truth presented by the doctor. Besides this there were some among them who knew God in the deeper experiences of saving grace.

There was "Mother Cobb," who for nearly fifty years had walked in the clear light of sanctifying grace. "Mother Cobb" was to a marked degree characterized by that peculiarity which is the inevitable result of the transforming power of grace. She was peculiar in disposition, in appearance and in conversation—so sweet in disposition you would at once forget the wrinkles in her face, and in appearance so neat that it seemed she would look so well in nothing else as she did in her blue calico dress and Quaker bonnet. Jesus in his saving power was the beginning and end of all her conversation. She allowed no opportunity for speaking a word for the Master to pass unimproved.

There was "Mother Combs," a power in exhortation, who possessed such a spirit of discernment that as she passed out of the church at the close of the first service held by the pastor at the beginning of the year, she unhesitatingly said, "He is a sinner," and subsequent events evidenced the truthfulness of the declaration; for before the year closed he was expelled for drunkenness.

There was "Mother Lawrence," a saint of God who gloried in the cross alone, and who, with Paul could truthfully exclaim, "whereby the world is crucified unto me and I unto the world." Good soul! when she heard of Doctor Redfield's preaching she seemed to sniff the battle from afar, and walked twelve miles across the prairies to attend the meetings.

And then there was my own mother—noble woman that she was—who had been true to the light she had received, but never came out into the experience of entire holiness until the first night of Doctor Redfield's meeting.

In the township of Hampshire, Kane county, Illinois, out about seven miles from Elgin, lived a pious widow who, at the death of her husband, was left with a small farm and a large family. Her son Joseph, just coming up into young manhood, was her main earthly reliance. One day the mother said to Joseph, "I wish you would arrange some seats in the kitchen, we are to have a meeting to-night." Joseph, supposing his mother had secured the services of the circuit rider, soon had the kitchen filled with extemporized seats and looked anxiously for the expected preacher. But when the hour for meeting arrived, judge of his surprise as his mother arose, Bible in hand, to commence the service. Several of the neighbors and quite a number of the young people had come in to attend the good widow's protracted meeting. Joseph was greatly chagrined, but out of respect to his mother, bore it as meekly as he could, hoping that this first meeting might be the last.   But to his dismay his mother gave out meetings for each evening of the week.   In answer to the prayers and faith of the pious mother, the Holy Spirit came down among the people in saving power.   Joseph was one of the first fruits of the revival.   And in after years, when he had grown up to manhood and had become mighty in the proclamation of the gospel, I have heard him with eyes streaming with tears and utterance choked with emotion, tell of his conversion in a protracted meeting held by his mother in her own kitchen.   When in January, 1858, Doctor Redfield was engaged in the meeting at Elgin, Joseph and several of the young people of the neighborhood drove down to hear him preach.   " There is a divinity which shapes our ends, rough-hew them how we will."   In these and subsequent meetings held by the doctor, this young man received an experience in the things of God and an inspiration of the Spirit which never left him.   And when the church was organized in the West he was one of the first to take his stand.   Under God he came to be a remarkable factor in the upbuilding of the cause, filling with credit and general acceptability almost every position the church had to offer; and besides other literary labors, writing the "Life of Redfield," a book which has proved a boon and a blessing to thousands.   Such was Joseph G. Terrill, a man who knew no envy and who was so free from anything like littleness of spirit that he could rejoice as sincerely at the preferment of a brother as he possibly could over his own advancement. Finally, as missionary secretary, early in the spring of 1895 he took a band of missionaries to New York to see them off for Africa, when he was suddenly taken with pneumonia and in a few days, at the home of a kind brother in the Lord, exclaiming, "I am prayed up to date and blessed up to date," he swept through the gates to his eternal reward.

C. E. Harroun was fully saved in the first meeting held by Doctor Redfield at St. Charles. He at once answered to the divine call and set about the work of preaching the gospel, and in all his after life he never could do anything else so well. For some years he preached at different points in Illinois and Wisconsin. He extended his labors to Iowa, Kansas and Missouri, and now in his declining years is assisting his son, C. E. Harroun, Jr., in building up a new conference in Oklahoma. In his ministrations he has, to a greater extent than any of his fellow laborers, both in pulpit and in altar work, retained the peculiar style and methods of Doctor Redfield. A fine singer, a powerful preacher, at times, as the Spirit moves him, congregations are aroused to a pitch of intense excitement.

CHAPTER II.

ON THE evening of Wednesday, February 3, 1858, Doctor Redfield began his labors in the Methodist Episcopal church at Marengo, Illinois. In the meetings which were going on for some weeks previous I had made a profession of religion, but I knew little of the conditions of saving faith. I remember as I went to the altar the preacher exclaimed, "That is a son of the covenant," referring, I suppose, to the fact that my parents were members of the church. A few prayers were offered, and at the close of the service the members gathered around, and, shaking my hand, expressed their delight that I had made up my mind to go to heaven. I was pleased to see them pleased and supposed I had religion. I was taken into the church on probation and assigned to a class. I remember that in class-meeting I would count around to see when it would come my turn to speak and fix up something in my mind to say, and when called on to speak would begin at the wrong end, get confused and sit down ashamed; and I thought this was bearing the cross.

I had some denominational pride, and on Wednesday morning I informed a friend of mine, a young lawyer, that we were to have a revivalist preach at our church and that he was considered a great preacher. He said he would like to hear him. I said, "I will call for you and we will go up to the church together." At the hour for service I found my young friend, and on the way up the street I began to have some misgivings and said, "This man is a stranger here and this first night he may be a little embarrassed. So little did I know about a man of God preaching the gospel. When we reached the church the house was crowded. My friend stopped by the door, but being a young convert I made my way through the congregation and took a seat on the pulpit steps. I shall never forget the service of that night. When the doctor, in his quiet, unassuming way, arose and announced the hymn beginning with the words, "Am I a soldier of the cross?" and at the end of the line in a quiet way, with rising inflection, repeated the words, "Am I?" it seemed as though each person in the congregation was silently putting the question to his own conscience—"Am I?" His manner and utterance in prayer were almost oppressive with reverence. When he announced his text— "And holiness without which no man shall see the Lord"—it seemed like eternity. In a quiet, conversational tone he spoke of the nature and necessity of scriptural holiness; with more emphasis and power he spoke of the conditions to be met in order to obtain the experience, and closed by relating some thrilling instances of the power of this grace in meetings he had held. He spoke perhaps for forty or forty-five minutes, and every person in the congregation seemed spell-bound. Sitting there on the pulpit steps I looked up at the man in amazement, and as he laid down the conditions necessary to the attainment of the experience I would say to myself, "That has never entered into my estimate of religion."

An odd character by the name of Bradley, who lived among the people and attended all the protracted meetings he could reach, made his appearance the first evening the doctor preached. As the congregation in almost breathless silence listened to the burning words of the preacher this man Bradley at the top of his voice suddenly cried out, "Glory! Hallelujah!" The doctor seeing the congregation was startled, looked in the direction the sound came from and quietly said, "Thank God you have one spiritual thermometer here," and went on with his discourse. The Holy Spirit that evening in an especial manner made individual application of truth. Several different members afterwards remarked, "I thought as he was preaching, I shall probably be the only one, but if he gives an opportunity I shall go forward." So when the invitation for seekers was given not only the altar but all the space in front and away down the aisles was filled.

A yonng Methodist girl by the name of Bishop, whose parents lived some seven miles out on Kishwauke Prairie, was boarding in town and attending the Presbyterian college. She was Methodist born and Methodist bred, a great stickler for the church, with special emphasis on THE, for it almost seemed to her there could be salvation in no other. Converted some five years before, she had come to consider no sacrifice too great for the upbuilding of the church. Working in festivals, singing in the choir, and leading penitents to the altar, were exercises in which her soul took especial delight, but she had never prayed audibly in a public congregation. Not that she had wilfully refused, but Satan had suggested that she had no talent for prayer and if she should attempt to pray in public she would make such a stuttering, stammering prayer it would disgrace the cause. So careful is the devil of God's cause. Several earnest prayers were offered, when the doctor said, "We will change the order of the meeting," and opportunity was given for testimony.

Miss Bishop in speaking told how earnestly she desired a religion that would save her. The doctor looked intently at the young woman as she was speaking and said, "Sister, wont you lead us in prayer?" A flash-light of conviction illuminated her soul and she exclaimed, "I never had religion enough to pray in a public congregation in my life, but I am going to to-night! Making her way to the altar, she fell on her knees and with increasing earnestness pleaded for the experience of a clean heart.

Back in the house an old man, familiarly known as Uncle Alf. S., who, either because he was not acquainted with the usages of the house of God, or because his mind was befogged by whiskey, had at the close of the invitation for seekers remained standing. He watched the young girl as in her earnestness she cried out, "I will have it. I will have it;" when, apparently in deep sympathy for the seeker, he suddenly cried out, "You shall have it." Then, becoming conscious of his surroundings, he sank back in the seat. At times as I have, in the hearing of that young woman, described this scene, she has responded—"AND THANK GOD, I GOT IT!"

Doctor Redfield was entertained at my father's house. On our return from the meeting he and I were alone in the sitting-room, when, turning to me, he inquired, "How did you like the meeting to-night?" I rather hesitatingly answered, "Oh, very well—a good deal of noise." The doctor said, "The noise didn't hurt you, did it?" I replied, "No; but there were some persons there who I thought might not like it." Suddenly he said, "Young man, has God Almighty made you ear-inspector-general of this town?" As meekly as I could I answered, "No, sir."

Up to the time of the doctor's arrival they claimed some sixty converts. The next day after the doctor's first sermon I don't think a dozen of them could have been found. One official member, a Universalist at heart, was greatly exercised over the discourage- ment of the young converts. But as the members sought and obtained the experience of entire sancti- fication conviction spread throughout the entire place and into the country for miles in every direc- tion. Doctors, lawyers and saloonkeepers were brought under the power of saving grace. As evi- dence of the genuineness of the work every saloon in the village was closed up. At the close of even- ing services men going in different directions to their homes could be heard shouting "Glory! Hallelujah!" And this at the time seemed no more out of place than it is ordinarily to hear men swear on the street.

People came in wagon loads from eight to ten miles, and in order to secure seats in the church often reached town before dark. One Mr. J., an avowed spiritualist, living out some seven miles, together with his partner in farm work, and their wives, were all grandly saved. Father and Mother Bishop, who held their membership on an adjoining circuit, although not yet fifty, thought themselves too old to get out to evening meetings. Hearing of the blessing experienced by their daughter, they came over and obtained the great salvation; and though their lives were prolonged into the seventies they were never afterward too old to attend night meetings. Some prominent men and church members had restitution to make, and a radical work of grace prevailed throughout the community. Mother Lawrence, who was all glorious within and whose soul, no doubt, like the king's daughter, was hung with jewels, was not outwardly particularly prepossessing, and during the preaching she had a peculiar way of drawling out A-man. Some of the members, who were anxious to have the work so respectable as not to disgust the Presbyterians and the Baptists, gave the old lady some pretty strong intimations to the effect that they would like to have her make herself conspicuous by her absence. At the close of the service one evening, the old lady told the doctor she thought on account of these things she might better go home. "Oh," said the doctor, "don't go, don't go; we can't spare you—we need at least one fog-splitter here."

Daniel B., the village drayman, a large, fleshy

man, who had little or no education, but who had
an abundance of good common sense, was unfortunately a victim of drink and at times fearfully pro-
fane. When Docter Redfield arrived in town the
checks were passed over to the drayman, who took
the baggage to my father's. The doctor inquired
how much the cartage would be, when B., hurrying
out of the room, replied, "Nothing, sir! Nothing,
sir!", He said to me afterwards, "I was glad to get
out of that man's presence. I was afraid I should
fall to the floor." Daniel was one of the early converts. He certainly proved to be a diamond in the
rough. Polished by grace, for years he shone for
God; and the last time he attended class he said,
"I want to be ready to go at the crack of the whip!"
The next day on the street attending to his work,
without a moment's warning, he dropped dead on
the walk and answered to the roll-call in the skies.

Mrs. C. was the wife of one of the most prominent lawyers in the county. Her name was on the
church book, but her heart was in the world. She
took pride in being a leader in fashion and worldly
pleasures. Attending the meeting she was brought
to face eternal consequences and was glad to humble
herself at the cross. The lawyer, proud of his young
wife as a butterfly of fashion, was greatly incensed
at the thought of her becoming, as he termed it. "a

Redfieldite." By entreaties and by threats he did all he could to dissuade her from being a true Christian. But the vow was passed beyond repeal and God had set the solemn seal. So, whether locked in the closet or pushed out on the door-step, she could shout and sing,

> "Where'er I am—where'er I move,
> I meet the object of my love."

In evidence of the spiritual momentum and force of this revival it may be sufficient to say, a daily five o'clock morning prayer-meeting was maintained in that church for more than a year. A large number of the most substantial people in the community were brought under the power of saving grace and many of them remained nobly true to the day of their death. I have been told that Doctor Redfield pronounced this revival the most thorough and perfect work in all his labors.

CHAPTER III.

FROM Marengo Doctor Redfield went to Woodstock, the county seat of McHenry county. The Methodists here were comparatively weak. They had no church building, but worshiped in a hall. The work at Woodstock met with great opposition from the very start, still much good was done. One prominent man who was saved became a local preacher and was afterwards elected sheriff of the county. Rev. B. was pastor. He was an inoffensive man, but took no decided stand.

One day in an afternoon meeting the doctor, addressing the pastor, said: "Brother B., do you enjoy the experience of entire sanctification?" Brother B. replied, "I can't say that I do." Brother B.," inquired the doctor, "when you joined the Rock River conference did you not say you was earnestly groaning to be made perfect in love?" Brother B. replied, "I did." The doctor said, "How long ago was that?" Brother B. answered, "Thirteen years ago." The doctor quietly, but with emphasis, said: "Brother B., isn't that a pretty long groan?" The pastor at once set about seeking the experience.

I. H. Fairchilds. a local preacher, got out into the
light at this meeting.   He figured quite prominently
in starting and building up the Free Methodist
church in that part of the state.   Meantime at St.
Charles "a king arose who knew not Joseph."   A
preacher by the name of Howard had been appointed
there.   He had but little sympathy for Methodism
in general, and especially abhorred and despised the
doctrine of entire sanctification.   He preached a
year or two in that vicinity for the Methodists, and
then went to the Universalists.   This man took a
very decided stand against those who had come out
under the labors of Doctor Redfield.   Perhaps the
pastor was not altogether responsible, for it was said
he consulted one of the leading bishops of the church
who advised him to the course he pursued.   The
Methodist church in the West, at this time, was in a
kind of intermediate state.   She had but little either
of religion or popularity.   The complete transition
took place in 1860, about the time of the breaking
out of the civil war, when, to a great extent, she sub-
stituted patriotism for salvation, and, courting the
smiles of the world, many of her preachers and
members united with Masonic lodges, and so with
her head in the lap of Delilah, as far as vital godliness was concerned, she was shorn of her strength.

The holiness movement in Western New York

was attracting a good deal of attention. A policy of proscription had been inaugurated, and under this rule an attempt was made to stamp out the work. The pastor at St. Charles, probably under instructions, pursued the same course there. Official members in sympathy with the doctrine and experience of holiness were removed from office, and many in good and regular standing, without judge or jury, were read out as withdrawn. During this administion the doctor returned to St. Charles. He was not allowed to occupy the Methodist pulpit, and his sympathizers procured an old unused Universalist church for him to preach in. That was a memorable Sabbath. The holiness people came in from all directions, and the house was crowded. Seymour Coleman, an old war horse of the Troy comference, was supplying the pulpit of the First Methodist Episcopal church of Aurora that year, and among those saved under his labors was one Benjamin Hackney. He was a man of fine appearance and of noble mind. He had enjoyed the distinction of representing his district in the State Legislature.

Brother Hackney and his devoted wife were at this Sunday morning service. In giving his testimony he spoke of the opposition and the tribulations which the true Christian must meet. This furnished the doctor with a text and a theme. At

the close of the love-feast he arose, and, reading the
closing words of the fourteenth verse of the seventh
of Revelation, "And he said to me, These are they
which came out of great tribulation, and have
washed their robes and made them white in the blood
of the Lamb," preached one of the most remarkable
sermons of his life. From this on the chasm wid-
ened, and finally these persecuted saints rented the
dining room of an old vacant hotel and fitted it up
for a place of worship, and, sending for Joseph
Terrill, the boy who was converted in his mother's
kitchen, they commenced a series of revival meetings which resulted in the salvation of a hundred
souls, the formation of a Free Methodist society
and the building of a church.

C. E. Harroun held revival meetings at Clintonville, now called South Elgin. A society was formed
there and a church built. During the year the work
on what was call Vermont street and at Franklinville
went on with increasing power. In harvest the men
would come in on their reapers late at night singing
and shouting the praises of God, then go over to the
school house for meeting. "And there was added
to the church daily such as were being saved." At
Franklinville church the preacher in charge got the
baptism and a hundred were converted or cleansed.
As to my personal experience that year I prefer to

let it, with all the mistakes and sins of my life, remain under the blood.

The work at the Franklinville church went on in power. But at a quarterly meeting held during the year the presiding elder warned the people against the use of dogmatic terms such as sanctification and the like. The preacher in charge began to tone down and finally took a decided stand against the work of holiness. When conference time came Father Bishop and others petitioned for a change of preachers. "For," said Father Bishop, "we will not pay Methodist preachers for fighting Methodist doctrine." The conference over, back came both the preachers—senior and junior—and now the battle was put in array in good earnest. Father Bishop opened his house for a Monday night holiness meeting, and from Woodstock, Queen Ann Prairie, Vermont street, Crystal Lake and the intervening country the holiness people rallied. The meeting was kept in the hands of the laity, and though the preacher came and proposed to lead it and finally informed the people that he would remove it to the church, he could not make his plans work. Souls were converted and sanctified at almost every gathering.

Living two or three miles east of Father Bishop was a family by the name of Best, and, as their name

indicates, they were to be classed among the super-
latively good. The family consisted of father, mother
and four boys. The boys were young, but were being
carefully taught and trained by the mother, who was
a woman of superior intelligence as well as of super-
lative piety. Outside of this family the neighborhood was wild and reckless. There had been no
preaching there for years, and many of the young
people had never heard a gospel sermon. The place
later became favorably known as "The Brick School
House." I. H. Fairchilds, the local preacher spoken
of before, sent an appointment to this school house
and a series of meetings was held. Many of the
holiness people attended, among them the Bishop
family, and as a result of the meetings floods of
mercy broke on the community and fifty or more
were saved. If I remember aright a Methodist
Episcopal class of forty was organized on an adjoining circuit as a fruit of this meeting. A good many
of the converts said they came to the meeting at
first to hear the Bishop girl shout. A good work
was going on and for a few Sabbaths Father Bishop
and family felt they ought to attend meetings at the
school house and did so. This served for a pretext
and they were soon cited to trial for not attending
public worship and class at Franklinville church
where they belonged. There were persons whose

names were on that church book who had attended neither public worship nor class for years, and some of whom were avowed Mormons, and others who gloried in being Universalists; but they were not troublers in Israel.

The day for the trial arrived and these people who were staunch Methodists, and who had come from Methodist stock a century old, appeared at the church. But they had hundreds of sympathizers, for they were well and favorably known throughout all that region. So on the day of the trial, to the dismay of the preacher the church was filled. Finally the preacher came in and informed the accused that he had concluded to have a private trial and to hold it in the parsonage across the street. Father Bishop, who knew something of Methodist law, quoted Baker on the discipline and said, "A trial should be private only at the request of the accused, and we demand a public trial; for," said he, "if we have done anything worthy of bonds or of death, we refuse not to be bound or to die." But the preacher took his committee and went over to the parsonage to go on with the trial, and the saints went on with a love-feast. As one after the other their heads went off, ecclesiastically, the preacher would come into the church and announce the fact.

William, the eldest son, in preparation for the

ministry had been attending the theological school
at Evanston.   When he went he took a church letter, but concluded not to put it in at Evanston, so on
his return home had it with him. When the preacher
declared him expelled William said, "Brother W.,
you can't expel me: I hold a letter." "Let me see
it," said the preacher, William feeling a little sus-
picious, held up the letter, when the preacher, as if
to get a better look at it, reached up, and, taking
hold of the corner where his own name was signed,
with a sudden jerk tore his name from the certifi-
cate.   At this a young woman by the name of Spon-
able with a piercing shriek, fell in a burden at the
feet of the preacher.   It was getting uncomfortably
warm for the pastor, and he started for the door;
but a stalwart saint stood against the door and refused to let him out.   He then rushed up into the
pulpit and with loud and earnest protestation, declared he did not tear the letter.   The saints looked
on him with pity and prayed the Lord to have
mercy on him.

Unjustly excluded from the church of their
choice they hardly knew what to do.   Finally
Father Bishop drew up articles of association, and
this family and many of their sympathizers formed
themselves into an Earnest Christian Band.   Most of
those whose names were on that paper have crossed

the flood, and those who remain are to the border come. "With charity for all and malice toward none" they still live to glorify God. I cannot begin to enumerate the remarkable events of those days. But not the least among them was the fact that one mother in Israel, with direct reference to the work of God, week after week refrained from taking food, and so, like the Mosaic and the gospel dispensations, the Holiness Movement in Northern Illinois in its beginning was characterized by a "forty day's fast."

CHAPTER IV.

THE WINTER following the meeting held by Doctor Redfield at Marengo, I was so convicted of my need of salvation I concluded I must be saved at any cost. In my desperation I went one day to the office of my young friend, the lawyer. I was so convicted I could not keep back the tears, and he, noticing my agitation, inquired the cause. I said to him, "Henry, it has come to this. I can go on as I am going, fill a drunkard's grave and go to a drunkard's hell, or I can give my heart to God, live to some purpose, die happy, and gain heaven;" then added, "and Henry, I shall do just as you say." He was a professed infidel; but, with a good deal of earnestness, he replied quickly, "Why get religion, of course." I replied, "That settles it."

That evening at the meeting in the church, I made my way to the altar and sought God in the pardon of my sins. I prayed earnestly, and Brother Wood, a local preacher, with others held on to God for me. Directly it seemed as if a single ray of sunlight streamed into my soul; rather faintly I said, "Hallelujah." The local preacher, thrusting his hand through

the altar railing, grasped mine and at the top of his
voice shouted, " Hallelujah!" The cloud broke, and
from my heart I began to sing,

> " This is the way I long have sought,
>   And mourned because I found it not."

From my earliest recollection a story had been
told me, which, when I seriously thought of seeking
God, would come up before me. The story was
that when I was born my maternal grandmother, a
good old New England Congregationalist, dedicated me to God and, naming me Edward Payson,
said I would be a minister of the gospel. I settled
that as I bowed at the altar in the church that night.
Not only so, but tobacco, and all my bad habits left
me as well. For weeks I shut myself up for study,
and only as I went to and from the church appeared
on the streets.

After consulting with my pastor I began to make
preparation to go to a school of the prophets over
on Lake Michigan and get fitted up to preach.
About three weeks after my conversion I went one
day to an afternoon meeting, feeling all through my
soul, I have lived up the grace I have received;
something more must be done for me. In speaking
I told the brethren and sisters just how I felt.
Mother Cobb, one of God's D. D.'s, jumped to her
feet and exclaimed. "The young man needs the ex-

perience of entire sanctification." I had seen a great
many in Doctor Redfield's meetings seeking the experience. I had seen their tears, witnessed their
earnestness and heard their groans; and, starting
down the aisle to the altar, I made up my mind "If
tears and groans and cries will bring it I will have
it." Falling on my knees with hands uplifted I began to cry out, "O Lord, sanctify me! Sanctify me!"
when the Holy Spirit, seemingly to get my attention,
began to whisper in my heart, "See here! See here!
You know God has called you to preach the gospel."
"Oh, yes," I replied, "I have settled that;" and then,
as if the Holy Spirit was to be put off with strong
crying and tears, again I cried, "Oh, Lord, sanctify
me! Sanctify me!" when as the Spirit for a little
gained my attention again he said, "You know God
has called you to preach the gospel. Will you start
out just as you are, and trust God for the qualfica-
tions?" I thought it over for a while. It looked to
me like failure; but I said, "Yes, Lord, you must take
the responsibility; I'll do the best I can."

Then came the suggestion, But suppose the Lord
should call you to leave friends and home and native
land, to go perhaps to leave your bones to bleach on
the burning sands of Africa, will you go? As these
tests were brought to bear on my heart I saw God
was not to be put off with strong crying and tears,

but demanded unconditional surrender. I cried,
"Yes, Lord, I'll go anywhere, be anything, or do
anything, only cleanse me." Just then faith took
hold in appropriating power and "the peace of God
which passeth understanding" took possession of my
soul. I arose from my knees and said, "Brethren
and sisters, I have been so honest in consecrating
myself that I dare stand before God in judgment
this moment." I knew that I was all given up, and
I knew that God knew I was. I looked at myself as
best I could from head to foot and said, "I am God's
man." Three days after I went to an afternoon
meeting. They were having a season of prayer. I
knelt at a front seat. The suggestion came that I
should pray. Then the thought came, "If you do,
the people sitting in the back of the church will look
you right in the face;" but I said, "I am God's man,"
and opened my mouth to pray; but before I could
utter a word down came the baptism of the Holy
Ghost and fire. God fulfilled to me the promise,
"Before they call will I answer, and while they are
yet speaking I will hear;" and for several hours I
could do nothing but shout the praises of God.

Just at dusk I returned home. Standing at the
gate at my father's house were three men, I at
once recognized them as Methodist brethren from a
near by neighborhood over north called the Burr

Oaks. They said, "We have been trying to hold a meeting in our schoolhouse, but have not been able to get a preacher to help us. We heard that God had saved you and thought we would come and see if you would come over and help us." I replied, "The Lord willing I will be there next Thursday night." I went, and have been going ever since. "What think ye of Christ?" were the first words from which I ever attempted to preach.

When I was converted I was secretary of a lodge of Freemasons. All my surroundings were favorable to Masonry. The next day after I was converted a prominent church member who was a Mason said to me, "A man needs to be a Christian in order to understand Masonry." But I never entered the lodge but once after my conversion, and went then to pay in some money that, as secretary, I had in my hands. Not that I was prejudiced against the order or had any light that it was wrong. I did not care to attend. The impulses of a regenerated heart are sometimes in advance of light on the understanding.

Some one may be ready to inquire, "Don't you believe in intellectual preparation for the work of the ministry?" Certainly I do. But, remember, there was then no Free Methodist church, no Free Methodist school. The needs of the work were urgent, and, in my case, for I relate my individual experience, I suppose the Lord saw it was better for me to start out even in my poverty of intellectual qualifications than to spend several years in preparation and perhaps become so rich in resources that I could preach independently of God. Certainly a liberal education is a good thing if consecrated to God. So wealth is a great blessing if consecrated to God. But ordinarily that is a tremendous *if.* I was naturally so independent that had there been anything this side of God and heaven on which I could lean I would have been almost certain at least to incline that way. Certainly let our young men in preparation for the work of the ministry attend the noble institutions with which, as a church, God has blessed us, and then let them go out, and, by the superiority of their work, demonstrate the utility of superior advantages.

David Cassady, my pastor, gave me verbal license to exhort, and in a short time I was duly licensed both as an exhorter and a local preacher. During the spring and summer I exercised my gifts, exhorting and preaching wherever I found an open door. I applied myself very closely to study, reading most of the standard works on Wesleyan theology. Timothy Benedict, who, after the expulsion of Rev. Vance, was appointed to fill out the year, when he left the charge told me when he heard that I was converted and was going into the ministry he would send me the complete works of Edward Payson as a foundation of a library. In due time the books arrived, and the sermons and writings of that man of God were of great benefit to me.

A blacksmith by the name of Hooker was converted in Doctor Redfield's meeting and was soon licensed as a local preacher. He was a social, good-natured man, with some natural talent but quite limited in acquired abilities. He and I labored together a good deal in meetings. I was naturally rather reserved, but my Brother H. never suffered from lack of confidence, At one time as we were engaged in a revival meeting we were entertained by a family of very intelligent, well-read Methodist people. Evenings at the close of meetings as we were seated around the fire Brother H. would invariably undertake to enlighten the family on points of theology and general information, but the most casual observer in listening to the conversation would at once discover that the family were much better informed than was the preacher. One evening as we retired to our room I expostulated with the brother and said to him, "These people are much better posted than we are." "I know," he replied, "but if you talk right up to them they will think you know as much as a bishop." The dear man came into the Free church at its beginning. He labored at Crystal Lake and some other points for a year or two with some degree of acceptability and undoubtedly accomplished some good. He enlisted and was elected captain of a company in the 105th Illinois Cavalry. His army life was brief. While out one day reconnoitering during the seven days' battle before Richmond he was shot through the body, and, becoming too weak to ride, his comrades assisted him to dismount. They placed him in a sitting position, with his back to a tree, and as the enemy was pressing them closely they were obliged to leave him to his fate. His eyes had already become glassy and the death damps were on his brow. Whatever service he may have rendered his country, had he remained in the service of the Lord, it undoubtedly had been better with his soul.

In the fall of 1859 Hooper Crews, presiding elder of Rockford district, took my name to the annual conference session and without passing any examination or even being present I was received into the Rock River annual conference on trial. I was appointed as junior preacher on the Lynnville circuit, lying some fifteen or twenty miles south of Rockford. Rev. Mr. Campbell was preacher in charge. He was not a member of the conference,

but an ordained local elder. He had traveled for
years as a colporteur and was good at selling books.
We were opposites in our manner and style of preaching. The old gentleman was slow and prosy and
like the bones in Ezekiel's vision, very dry. I was
full of zeal, in fact had a good deal more zeal than
judgment. At the east end of the circuit we had an
appointment in what was known as the Kendrick
schoolhouse, so called from a family of that name
who lived near by. And if ever a saint wrestled
with God in prayer for souls Aunt Polly Kendrick
certainly did. Securing the services of my friend,
Hooker, I held a series of meetings at this schoolhouse. We had a number of converts and several
were added to the class. The converts came out on
the fire line and were quite demonstrative. Brother
C. and I preached once in two weeks alternately.
When he came to preach he was quite annoyed
by the demonstrations and the noise. In order to
correct what he seemed to consider extreme in this
direction he would inform the people that empty
wagons always made the most noise. Then on my
round I would tell them if they would load up with
the world, the flesh and the devil, their carts would not
make much noise. Being naturally diffident it was
a great embarrassment to go to the houses of my
members to stop, and I would frequently drive

home to my father's, nearly thirty miles, rather than trouble the people.

Aunt Polly Kendrick had quite a family of children who are now scattered far from the old homestead. One son, who at the time of which I write was not yet born, is now a district elder in the Susquehanna conference of our church. Hooper Crews, my presiding elder, was very kind and did what he could to advise and encourage me in the work. He was a fine type of the old Virginia gentleman and a strong man in the pulpit.

Early in the summer of 1860 I arranged for a grove meeting at Lynnville. I engaged Seymour Coleman to assist, and as there was no very direct railroad communication I sent a two-seated covered carriage across the country to Aurora for Brother Coleman and wife. When they arrived a gentleman, a stranger to me, was seated in front with the driver. When the formalities of meeting were over Brother Coleman turned and said, "This is Brother Travis, one of our local preachers from Aurora whom I took the liberty to invite to accompany us." I welcomed Brother Travis and we soon set the battle in array. Seymour Coleman was noted for his quaint way of expressing himself. As one person at this meeting said to me, "He talks so handy." A great crowd came out on Sunday. We had a grand love-feast, and just about time for the preaching service the heavens gathered blackness and it seemed every moment as though the storm would break upon us. Father Coleman kneeled down for the opening prayer and cried out, "O Lord, keep back the storm until thy servant has delivered his message!" It was a solemn and impressive scene—that old veteran of giant frame, with snow-white locks falling around his massive brow, in the very face of the frowning heavens asking God to hold the elements in check that he might declare his word. But the God of Elijah heard and answered his servant's prayer. Taking the sixth and seventh verses of the ninth of Isaiah for his text, he preached one of the most remarkable sermons on the divinity of Christ to which I ever listened. Reaching the climax, in demonstration of the divinity of Jesus, in his characteristic way he cried out, "There! there is no old God and his boy about that!"

As the sermon closed we needed no prophet to warn us as Ahab of old was warned, "Prepare and get thee down that the rain stop thee not," for no sooner had we reached shelter than the rain poured in torrents. But the heavens were not much blacker than was the face of the wife of the hotel keeper, a bold, forward woman who knew neither shamefacedness nor sobriety. She was a Unitarian Universalist, and Father

Coleman had completely annihilated her pet theory. Several of the friends from Marengo, were present and assisted at the services and an influence went out from the meeting which told largely for good all over the circuit.

CHAPTER V.

THE grove meeting spoken of in the last chapter was held about the first of June, 1860. I was not married, and at this time was boarding with a very pleasant Methodist family by the name of Jennings. I took Brother Travis to my room, and he enjoyed the hospitality of this kind family. On Monday morning as I was arranging the conveyance for the return of Brother and Sister Coleman to Aurora, Brother Travis informed me that he was to remain and assist a Brother McGilvary, a Wesleyan Methodist preacher, on his circuit. I had no thought but what he would be obliged to return home at the close of the meeting, and was taken by surprise, but at once said, "If you can stay longer you certainly must stop with me." Brother Travis very readily consented to this, and informed the Wesleyan brother he had concluded to stay and assist Brother Hart.

One morning Brother Travis took up the *Northwestern Christian Advocate* and his eye fell on the notice of a camp-meeting commencing the next week, to be held in Wisconsin. As he read the notice aloud to me he said, "This notice is signed by George Fox,

P. C. I don't know the man, but I like the ring of the notice, suppose we attend the meeting." I said, "Very well, I will get my appointments filled for a few Sabbaths and we will attend this meeting, and then drive down and take in the laymen's camp-meeting at St. Charles, Illinois." At this time I was driving a little sorrel Morgan mare. She was low built and heavy, and there seemed to be no limit to her powers of endurance. I could drive her sixty or seventy miles in a day, and at the end of the journey if no hay was to be had she seemed just as thankful for hazel brush. Early in the morning we hitched up "Pet" and started north. We drove to Beloit, and the first night stayed with the Methodist parson. Getting an early start, we struck out the next day for Janesville. When about twenty miles north of Beloit we espied a jack standing in a pasture and demurely gazing over the fence into the road. I noticed that my pony was a little skittish, but urged her along; when, just before we reached the beast he gave one of those horrible brays for which such animals are eminent, and the pony whirled like a flash and cramped and tipped the buggy just enough to land Brother Travis and myself, together with the robes, grips, etc., in the dust.

The country was quite rolling, and by the time we could gather ourselves up the horse and buggy

were disappearing over the summit of a hill. Brother
Travis seemed to consider it quite a joke, but I
thought to myself, "You may laugh, but the outfit
belongs to me." Picking up blankets and grips, etc.,
we started back after the fleeing horse. We walked
perhaps a mile when we discovered a team coming
with a horse and buggy following. I soon saw by a
peculiar way she had of tossing her head that it was
my pony. It seems she had become tired of running,
and when the man with the team met her she was
walking leisurely along, and the man, concluding she
belonged to somebody in the direction she came
from, hitched her behind his wagon and brought her
to us. We thanked the man for his kindness, and
when on examination I found that no damage had
been done but that everything was intact, I laughed
too.

Late at night after a long day's drive we reached
the camp-ground. We found Brother Fox, and he
arranged for our entertainment. The presiding
elder had charge of the meeting, and in the morning
he questioned us as to who we were, and I informed
him that I was a member on trial in the Rock River
conference and junior preacher on the Lynnville circuit, and that Brother Travis was a local preacher
from the Aurora charge. That evening the elder,
I presume because I was a conference preacher, put

me up to preach. I did the best I could, but no great degree of enthusiasm was awakened, and at the close no one came up to congratulate me on the success of my effort. When Brother Travis and myself got alone he said, "You have spoiled my chances for preaching here, and I don't think you will have another opportunity." And true enough, neither of us was called on to preach after that. The elder gave us quite a severe letting alone, for I presume he had heard of the Redfieldites and concluded that I at least was badly tinctured.

Leaving the camp-ground, we started southeast for the laymen's camp-meeting. On our way we took in Marengo and stayed one night at my father's. When he learned that I was going to the camp-meeting he was greatly exercised, and taking me one side said he would give me a hundred dollars if I would not go. I told him I wanted to see for myself and had decided to go. Driving along the next day, Brother Travis was full of inquiries about these people, for he had concluded from what he had heard of them that they were a rough, boisterous set, with little or no culture or refinement.

We were late in starting from Marengo and it was late at night when we reached Saint Charles, so we decided to stop for the night at the hotel in the village and go to the ground in the morning. Early on

Friday morning we drove on to the camp-ground.
There was a large circle of tents in one of the finest
groves for camp-meeting purposes I ever saw. The
grove belonged to Brother J. M. Laughlin. Their
large dwelling stood near, and on such occasions as
this they kept "open house." I was acquainted with
nearly all the tent-holders, and so introduced my
traveling companion. Brother Travis greatly desired
to meet Doctor Redfield, so I looked him up and
gave him an introduction. I excused myself and
left them together. About two hours after, meeting
Brother Travis, I inquired how he liked Doctor Redfield. Evincing, for him, a great degree of enthusiasm, he replied: "Why, I learned more theology in
two hours' conversation with that man than I ever
knew before." They soon had Brother Travis up to
preach. He had given me to understand very distinctly that he never would leave the Methodist
Episcopal church to go with this people. Judge of
my surprise, then, when I heard him, as he warmed
up in his sermon, exclaim, "If you will take me I
will join you and go wherever you send me." He
was received and sent to Saint Louis, Missouri.

Here for the first time I met Rev. B. T. Roberts.
He was about thirty-seven years of age and in the
prime of his manhood. With a Roman cast of countenance, high, full forehead surrounded with hair

black as a raven's wing, I thought he was one of the finest looking men I had ever seen. The meeting was well under way when we reached the ground, and certainly there seemed to be no one at all disposed to "hold" it. That there was much of divine power manifested no one could question, and that there was a good deal of the rankest fanaticism no one in his right senses could deny. Someone inquired of Father Seymour Coleman about some of the extravagant demonstrations. The old gentleman replied, "The fact is, these people have suffered so much from ecclesiastical bondage in the churches that now they are free they are like young colts let loose and don't know how to act." Like the indulgences of Tetsel of old, gifts were on the market, but to be dispensed without money and without price. Doctor Redfield had the general oversight of the meeting, but the most he would do was in a good natured way to speak out from the stand, "If the devil tells any of you to stand on your head, don't do it." But the good Lord knew that the people were honestly seeking to be right, and in his love and mercy he let showers of blessing fall on them.

The camp-meeting went on with increasing power. One day as the testimony meeting was at a high tide Doctor Redfield called out from the stand, " Mattie, sing Gideon," when the Bishop girl, stepping out

into the aisle, in a strong, clear voice began to
sing :

> "See Gideon marching out to fight,
> See Gideon marching out to fight,
> See Gideon marching out to fight,
> He had no weapon but a light.
> If you belong to Gideon's band,
> Here's my heart and here's my hand,
> We're fighting for a home."

Before the first verse was finished the camp-
ground was in an uproar of excitement, and the slain
of the Lord were many. There were many instances
of remarkable conversions at this meeting, and many
entered into the experience of entire sanctification.
Quite a number were present from Saint Louis.
These represented the work raised up by Doctor
Redfield in that city.

During this meeting the first convention in connection with the work in the West was held on a rail
pile near Brother Laughlin's house. The work was
all in a formative state, and the preachers had to
depend largely on raising up their own circuits. I
stated to the convention that I felt I ought to remain
on my charge until fall, and then if they had any
work for me I would be ready to take it. Brother
Travis went from the camp-ground to his new field
in Saint Louis, and I returned to my circuit. I
labored on until about the first of August, when,
having fully decided that "It is not good that man

should be alone," on the ninth day, of August, 1860, with a few invited friends, I made my way to a cozy farmhouse on Kishwaukee Prairie, where at about six p. m., Rev. I. H. Fairchilds officiating, the marriage ceremony was performed, and the Bishop girl as such lost her identity and henceforth in these papers will be referred to as my wife. Or the two made one may be known, not by the editorial, but by the plural personal pronoun we.

The next Sabbath found us on the circuit and at the morning appointment. I suspect the good lady by whom we were entertained thought the young preacher's wife was most too plainly attired for a bride, for she made several suggestions as to her dress and did what she could to make her presentable to the congregation; "for," said she, "you know they will all be looking at you." We got along without any great degree of embarrassment. I preached the best I could, and by the time my wife was through with her exhortation fashion plates had passed out of mind.

One Sabbath not long after this we reached Lynnville. The hotel keeper's wife was out, and at the close of the service gave expression to some very decided remarks in criticism of my sermon. "The fact is," she said, "when you get out of matter and don't know what to say you pitch on to the Universalists. I want you to understand I have seen Universalists die, and they are just as good as anybody." When the woman closed her tirade my wife struck up and sang, "I am glad salvation is free," and I closed with the benediction. As the woman passed out of the house she was heard to say, "If I had known they would take it that way I wouldn't have said anything."

At the close of the conference year we returned to Marengo. I wrote my presiding elder to have my name discontinued. I took my letter from the church and wrote to Aurora, where it was understood I was to be appointed, that I was ready to come. But the brethren there were very anxious to have Seymour Coleman, who had labored so successfully there in the Methodist Episcopal church and seemed almost decided to cast in his lot with them, take the charge. So we were without work, and, so far as we could see, without any immediate prospect of having any. My parents were opposed to my leaving the Methodist Episcopal church, and now that no way was open for us in the new church, were well convinced that we were out of the divine order. In our strait my wife and myself laid the matter before the Lord and decided we would step into the first open door. The new presiding elder on his way from conference stopped at my father's. He informed us that Elder

Crews held my letter till the last day of the session, hoping I would change my mind. The elder told what a fine circuit they had me down for, and then said, "I want you to hold yourself in readiness, for I shall have work for you the second quarter if not the first." And so it began to look as though we had made a mistake and must retrace our steps.

CHAPTER VI.

THE fall of 1860 was a time of great political excitement. The country was on the verge of the great rebellion. The darkened horizon and the muttering thunder told of the fearful storm which was to break on the land. Mr. Lincoln was the candidate of the Republican party and Mr. Douglas and others represented different phases of the Democracy. Senator Hale, of New Hampshire, was advertised to speak in the park at Marengo, and I went down to hear him. On my return I stepped into my father's store to write, and while standing at the desk three men came in, one of whom I recognized as a Brother Merriman, of Garden Prairie. He gave me an introduction to the others, one as David Cooper and the other as John Horan, both of Belvidere. These men were good types of the intelligent, uncompromising Irish gentleman. Mr. Cooper at once said, "We have come to see if we can get you to go to Belvidere to preach." I replied, "Yes, sir; will you be ready for me by next Sunday?" He seemed a little taken aback, and said, "No, not quite as soon as that, but we will be ready by the following Sabbath." "Very well," I replied, "I have an appointment next Sunday morning at Garden Prairie. Come up to that and let me know how you succeed in getting a place," etc. They agreed to this, and returned to Belvidere. Brother Cooper told me afterwards that he was greatly surprised at my ready response to his request. He said he thought I would make some inquiries at least as to support. He did not understand the state of mind I was in, and that I at once recognized this as the first open door.

The next Sabbath Brothers Cooper and Horan were at Garden Prairie, and reported that they had secured an old vacant Universalist church for our meeting. Brother Cooper had attended a grove meeting held by Brother Roberts at Bonus Prairie immediately after the Saint Charles camp-meeting. He professed religion, but his grace was strongly of the combative sort. Mr. Horan made no profession. At the appointed time the following Sabbath morning we were at the church ready for action. By some mistake Lucius Matlack, a prominent Wesleyan Methodist preacher, and myself had appointments in that same house at the same hour. As Mr. Matlack took in the situation he quite decidedly stated that he did not care to occupy the position of a contestant for a pulpit, and withdrew. I went on with my meeting, and gave notice that Doctor Redfield would preach there that evening. At night the house was crowded and the doctor preached one of his characteristic sermons, the last I ever heard him preach that was at all like himself. In about a week after he was stricken with paralysis, and as far as preaching was concerned his labors were at an end. We drove across the country with the doctor and his wife to Ogle county, where the doctor preached in a schoolhouse where Brother Terrill had already organized a class. From there he went on his way to Aurora, where, at the home of Rev. Judah Mead, he was disabled.

Brother Terrill had raised up a good class in Ogle county. J. W. Dake sold out his farm and went into the work, and in a few years had all his earthly possessions invested in heavenly stock. U. C. Rose, a physician, soon commenced preaching, and Sylvester Forbes, quite an eccentric character, became prominent in the work both in Illinois and in Michigan. A church was built at Ogle Station and several powerful camp-meetings were held in the vicinity. The members became scattered. The Martins went to Kansas and settled near Osborne City, and a circuit was raised up in that county. We held on for a while in the Universalist church at Belvidere and then rented a vacant Congregationalist church, which was in a better locality and much more convenient.

In a few weeks I decided to hold special revival services. I had my plans laid to get Doctor Redfield to assist when I needed help in revivals, but now that the doctor was laid aside I was thrown back on the Lord.

We commenced the meeting and soon quite an interest was awakened. The friends came from Marengo and vicinity, and the house became altogether too small to accommodate the crowds. Father Collier, an old English class-leader, and others took their stand and the work moved on in power. Prominent ladies would come at an early hour for the evening meeting, and, finding the door locked, in their eagerness to get in and secure a seat would raise the sash of the window and climb from the platform into the house. Brother Harroun assisted in the meetings for a while, and Brother Wood, the local preacher from Marengo, rendered efficient service. I do not remember just the number of converts, but if my memory is not at fault I organized a society of fifty or more. I took in some of the scattered ones around Marengo, and here I received my wife into the church; for although we had not yet received the Discipline we were beginning to be known as Free Methodists.

Not long after this I attended a meeting at Clintonville, where the Discipline was formally adopted.

We soon bought the church building in which we worshiped. We labored on until the following summer, when James Mathews came on from the East and took the work. Since that time the work at Belvidere has passed through severe testings and has had times of sifting, but I believe the fire has never been entirely extinguished on its altar. A class was organized at Garden Prairie and also one on Bonus Prairie.

Many of the friends at Marengo had expressed a desire for a meeting at that point; so, with our labors concluded at Belvidere, I informed them I was ready to go to their help. But now when the test had come it appeared to them to be assuming quite a responsibility to step out of a strong, well-appointed organization into an embryo church not yet fairly out of the shell. I at once took in the situation, and, in order to save them from embarrassment and myself from the charge of proselyting, I did not ask anyone to become responsible for hall rent, but took advantage of the pleasant evenings of June and commenced meetings in the street. Street meetings were a new feature in that section, and on Sunday nights we soon had large congregations, the people driving in from the country to witness the novel scene. The Lord was so manifestly in the movement that the good brethren were not slow to fall in line and authorized me to engage Metropolitan Hall, the largest hall in town, for our meetings.

Judah Mead, of Aurora, had joined our people and was acting as chairman over the work. I sent for him to come and hold a quarterly meeting for me. We had a memorable prayer-meeting on the Saturday evening of that occasion. It was a very warm evening, and up in the hall, with windows overlooking the town thrown wide open, a sound went forth that to some of the people seemed almost enough to wake the dead. My father especially, who was a class-leader and quite a stickler for the old church, was greatly exercised and felt himself forever and irretrievably disgraced. On Sunday morning we had a grand love-feast, and at the close of the communion service I had thought to organize a class, but being a little doubtful as to a very general response I concluded to transfer my Vermont street class, organized some time before, to Marengo, and announcing the fact of transfer I said, "We now nave a Free Methodist church in Marengo, and if any wish to unite they can now have the opportunity." Brother E. G. Wood, my local preacher friend, my mother, Sister Coon and Sister Minerva Barron stepped out, answered the questions of the Discipline, and were duly voted in. Others soon followed.

One Sunday morning Daniel B., the village drayman, came into meeting and in his quaint way announced his determination to go with us. Brother
B. was sexton at the cemetery, and this was about
the way in which he made known to us his desire to
unite: "Oh," said he, "how mean I have been! As
I was praying over the matter of church relation I
told the Lord that wherever he blessed me there
should be my home. I came here to meeting and
got so blessed that as I went out into the burying-
ground hallelujahs as big as hogsheads rolled all
around me, and then I didn't join. Now if you'll
take me I want to join to-day."

We bought a centrally located lot, moved back
the old building standing on it, tore out the parti-
tions, made some seats, and had a room which would
accommodate about two hundred. In this room we
held meetings through the winter; at times it was
packed almost to suffocation. In the spring we
began the erection of a church, and when completed
we moved in with a membership which, as near as I
remember, numbered about one hundred. It was
during the building of this church that Marengo was
visited with a fearful tornado, which carried death
and destruction in its track. We got the people
together that evening in our place of worship, and
with the assistance of Brother Frank Shepardson,

who was with us, we were able to exhort the people to repentance and salvation, from the words "The wages of sin is death, but the gift of God is eternal life through Jesus Christ our Lord."

That fall I was sent by conference to Saint Charles, Geneva, Batavia, Wheaton, etc. Borrowing Doctor Redfield's horse and two-seated carriage, I took my wife and our four weeks' old baby girl and bidding good-by to the friends at Marengo we made our way to our new field of labor. It was a large circuit, but we had considerable help. William Morrison, our "sweet singer in Israel," and other local preachers rendered efficient aid; besides, we had a junior preacher sent by conference. I don't remember his name, but his manner of preaching can never escape my memory. He would soar so high that all good effect of his preaching was lost on the congregation in the fearful apprehension as to his ever being able to get safely down to earth again.

CHAPTER VII.

PERHAPS a chapter made up of incidents in connection with the work at Belvidere and Marengo may be of interest and profit.

Mr. Horan took a lively interest in the work at Belvidere, and finally presented himself at the altar for prayers. We prayed for him and urged him to pray, but could not prevail on him to open his mouth. Afterwards, in conversation with him at his house, he said, "Mr. Hart, if my salvation depends on my praying aloud at the altar I cannot be saved. Not that I have any objection to it, but I simply cannot." I replied: "Mr. Horan, before you get blessed I think you will pray."

He was switchman at the depot and attended to making up the trains. One cold morning, the ground covered with snow and ice, as he was switching cars he attempted to jump on to the rear end of a train which was backing down to a switch, when his feet slipped and he fell between the tracks under the train. The train was not moving very rapidly, but he knew if he remained there until the engine should reach him, it being so much nearer the ground, he would be crushed to death. By a great effort he threw himself out between the wheels of the moving train and escaped with his feet badly mangled. They conveyed him at once to his home. The surgeon came, dressed his wounds, and made him as comfortable as he could. I was then sent for. I made my way to the house, and as I entered the room I found him bolstered up in a large chair, his feet resting on cushions. As he caught sight of me he reached out his hand, and with a good deal of emotion cried out, "O, Mr. Hart, if there had been five hundred men around that train they would have heard me calling on God for mercy!"

A lady who had been converted in the meeting came forward one evening to seek the experience of a clean heart. As she was going through with her consecration, amid her sobs and groans she would cry out, "Oh, how can I give her up? How can I give her up?" My wife, kneeling by her side, said, "Sister, lay all on the altar." Turning to my wife, with deep feeling she said, "It seems to me if I put my little girl on the altar that God will take her out of the world." The only reply was, "Sister, lay all on the altar." Finally she cried out, "It is done; she is the Lord's."

That consecration was tested, for in a few weeks I was called upon to preach the funeral sermon of that little girl. I never shall forget as that mother stood beside the open coffin and for the last time looked on the marble-like features of her dead child, how, with uplifted eyes as she looked through the blinding tears, in tones of triumph she cried, "The Lord gave, and the Lord hath taken away; blessed be the name of the Lord." You may say, "It is hard thus to consecrate and dedicate our loved ones to the Lord." But what did the grace of God do for that mother? I answer, it prepared her for the trial. The severing of the tenderest cords of our nature— the snapping of heart-strings—must sooner or later come; and God in his mercy proposes to prepare us for the test.

In our first meeting at Marengo a resolute woman by the name of Church was soundly converted and became an active worker. She had some sons who were exceptionally bright. She learned that one of her boys was frequenting the only saloon with which the village was ornamented. One day she visited the establishment, and finding her boy there led him to the door. Then, stepping back, she took the broom and literally swept the shelves and bar clean. Demijohns and bottles came down with a crash, and the contents were past gathering up. She never was prosecuted, for Lawyer Coon, whatever else he was or was not, was a good temperance advocate, and he assured her he would defend her. She seemed to be possessed of a spirit akin to that by which Mrs. Nation of Kansas is being impelled. But what about her movement? Do you know that when moral sensibilities become benumbed and Satan is having things about his own way the Lord sometimes stirs up someone to deeds, which from the standpoint of human selfishness, and which, judged by the standard of unjust human laws, seem to be extreme and altogether out of place? Take, for instance, the cases of Gideon and of Samson; the heroes of Boston Harbor in the destruction of the tea; and in later years that of John Brown. I don't know but in these days of criminal apathy with reference to the liquor traffic the Lord is stirring this woman to deeds of noble daring. I earnestly pray that in all except the hanging she may prove to be the John Brown and forerunner of emancipation from the power of King Alcohol; that in all except the beheading she may prove to be the John the Baptist and herald of the gospel of universal prohibition.

The first year I was on the Marengo work, Garden Prairie and other points were included in the circuit. J. W. Dake was junior preacher. Brother Dake was fresh from the farm, and being naturally diffident under the most favorable circumstances it was a

great cross for him to attempt to preach. One Sabbath I was to be away and told Brother Dake he
must take the Sunday evening appointment in the
street at Marengo. The time for the street service
arrived, but Brother Dake could not be found. The
cross was so heavy the poor man hid himself that he
might not be found and taken to the meeting. A
Brother F., a local preacher, was present and talked
the best he could. Lawyer Coon, although greatly
incensed because his wife would shout and sing and
pray, seemed to have an underlying desire for the
success of our work. Quite a number of times in my
financial straits he manifested this desire in render-
ing me material aid. That Sunday evening the
lawyer was in the congregation. At the close of the
service in a petulent tone he exclaimed, "Hart was
away, Dake didn't come, and F. tried to preach,"
and, making some ridiculous remark, turned away.
I don't think Brother Dake ever attempted to dodge
the cross after that.

After the Discipline with its rule forbidding connection with secret societies came out, I began more
closely to investigate the subject of secrecy. I became thoroughly convinced that oath-bound secret
societies were wrong, both in principle and in practice. So I not only abstained from connection with
the lodge, but in organizing societies I gave the

grounds on which we objected to secretism and reasons for the rule in our book of discipline. Of
course this subjected me to labor, and I was waited
on by the master of the lodge, who informed me that
a special meeting had been called for the following
Wednesday evening, and requested me, with others
who were delinquent in the payment of dues, to be
present. I informed him I would either be there or
write them a letter. I wrote them a letter and stated
to them that I had consecrated myself, with all the
powers of my being, to the advancement of the
kingdom of the Lord Jesus Christ; that after careful
investigation I was convinced that Masonry, both in
principle and in practice, was in opposition to that
kingdom, and that as an honest man I could have
nothing more to do with it. I closed in Masonic
language by saying, "You can take due notice hereof
and govern yourselves accordingly." Not long after
I received a notice informing me that I was expelled
for non-payment of dues and other gross unmasonic
conduct. I was tempted and considerably perplexed.

One day I went down town, and seeing the village
drayman, who was a member of the order, ran out
and jumped on to the dray and told him what I had
received and how I felt. He at once inquired,
"What of it?" I answered, "You know it is a powerful order, and as I am going out to preach if they

are so disposed they can do me great injury." With
a look of surprise he inquired, "Where is your faith
in God?" In my anxiety I had failed to view the
matter in this light. But that settled it with me.
Not. many days after in passing along the street I
met the drayman, and by a nod of the head he mo-
tioned me to his side. As I stood by him, in his
quaint way he said, "Brother Ed., I didn't think it
would make a feller feel so." I said, "What's the
matter, Brother Dan?" "I have got one of them ar'
notices," he replied, "and they are crowding me on
bills I am owing and making it warm for me." I
answered, "All I can say to you is what you said to
me, 'Where is your faith in God?'" and left him.
In a few days I met him again. His great fat face
was in a broad grin, and he exclaimed, "It's all
right! It's all right!" "Ah!" I inquired, "how is
that?" He replied, "You know old Mr. Smyth died
over north?" "Yes." "Well, I was digging the
grave to-day, and as I dug I kept thinking over the
matter of that notice, and when I had finished the
digging I made a hole about six inches deep in the
bottom of the grave, and putting the notice in the
hole covered it up, and getting down on my knees
called on God for victory, and I got it. And now,"
said he, "it's buried in the bottom of old Mr. Smyth's
grave and it will never come up till the resurrection."

CHAPTER VIII.

At about the beginning of our work at Marengo I preached one Sabbath evening on the street from the text, "Blessed are the pure in heart, for they shall see God." In the hotel across the way, in one of the front rooms, was lying a man very low with typhoid fever. He was a grain buyer. He and his brother were in business together. The brother was not married, but the one of whom I write had a wife and one child, a bright boy of about three years. The wife and child were on a visit East when the father was taken sick, and at the time of this street service had not returned. The sick man heard the text, if not the sermon. Becoming dangerously ill the wife and child were sent for, and on their arrival he was removed to their own home in the village.

Early one morning a messenger came hurriedly for my wife and myself, saying that Mr. Blandon was beyond all hope of recovery, and was very anxious to see us. We made our way to the house, and found him lying in a bedroom on the first floor. The window was open, and standing around and peering in were several of his associates, anxious to learn of his condition. This man, while outwardly moral, was one who seldom, if ever, attended the house of God, and one who to all appearance never had a serious thought about the salvation of his soul. As he caught a glimpse of us as we entered the room he called out eagerly, "Oh, pray for me! pray for me!" I said to him, "Certainly we will, but our prayers cannot save you, you must pray for yourself." "Oh," said he, "I don't know how to pray." I said, "Then repeat a prayer after me." And repeating the simplest form of prayer I could, "God be merciful to me a sinner," he would say it over after me with all the emphasis he could command. Weeping and sobbing his wife, leading the child, came into the room. As he saw her he cried out, "O wife, teach my boy to read the Bible and to pray!" His brother coming in he said to him, "O brother, we have been after gold, gold, but none but the pure in heart can see God." Every little while saloon-keepers and other hard men would reach in through the open window, and pulling my coat, inquire what I thought about his chances for salvation.

We talked and prayed with him the best we could, and finally came the confession: "When I was thirteen years old, my mother died and I kneeled at her bedside and promised to give my heart to God and meet her in heaven." We stayed by his side until about the time he passed away. We had hope in his death, for we believe God had mercy on him and saved him. According to his dying request I preached the funeral sermon in the Methodist Episcopal church to a large congregation. I do not know that I ever realized more of the presence of God than was manifested in that house on that occasion. I used for a text Deuteronomy 32:11, 12.

Twenty years after, in preaching in a revival meeting in San Jose, California, by way of illustration I related the above incident, giving the name of the place where it occurred, but not the name of the person. At the close of the service an old sister by the name of Wallace said to me, "Marengo, Illinois? Why, I had two nephews by the name of Blandon there." I said to her, "The person to whom I referred in the incident was Granger Blandon." "Oh," she said, "he was my sister's son. She was a devoted saint of God and wrestled with God in prayer for her sons, and said that she had the witness that he would save them." In the case of this one at least after a lapse of perhaps twenty years the mother's prayer was answered.

We spent a pleasant year at Saint Charles, most of our work, however, by way of special effort being put in at Geneva. We held revival services in the old courthouse. At first the work moved rather slowly.

One day the recording steward told me that the official board at one of its meetings had passed a resolution declaring that the Lord does not now heal diseases in answer to prayer as in former times. The steward said he had become ashamed of the action and had torn the leaf on which it was recorded from the book. But the action stood, and feeling that such a blow at faith in God would paralyze all our efforts, I called the board together and told them that they must rescind their action or I should stop the meeting. They readily complied with my request and rescinded the action, and the work at once began to move with power.

A German man and wife named Schones were clearly saved. They had been Catholics, but by degrees their eyes had been opened to the errors of that system. At one time Brother Schones went to the priest to get him to baptize his child, who was lying at the point of death. He found the priest feasting and drinking wine, and although he proposed to get a carriage and pay him well besides the priest refused to go. So Brother Schones went home, and in his desperation baptized the child himself, and said, "Lord, that must do." Gradually he lost faith in Catholicism, and when our meeting began came and stood in the stairway, and listening to the preaching was brought to feel his need of salvation. He came to the penitent form and was clearly saved. He then stayed with the children and sent his wife to the meeting. She could not understand English, but he told her when I got through preaching and they were singing to go up and kneel at the bench in front. So up she came, and kneeling straight up on her knees got out her prayer-book and read over her prayers as fast as ever she could. As she could not understand English we could not give her much instruction, but finally in prayer I cried out, "O Lord! let the light on this poor woman's heart." And she afterwards told us, for she learned to speak English a little, that when I cried out the light came to her heart.

After their conversion we stopped at their house during the remainder of the meeting. Crucifixes and beads were given to the children for playthings, and these happy converts went directly by faith to Jesus for grace and help. While stopping with them our babe was quite sick, and we were a good deal concerned, fearing she might die, and the good woman would console us in words about like these, "Oh, don't cry; ven our first baby was shick I criedt and Mr. Schones he criedt, but the next von I criedt but

Mr. Schones he not cry, and de next one I don't cry neider. Oh! you haf more before you haf less." These words were true and the prophecy was fulfilled. For some years they walked in the light, but, I believe, were finally drawn off to rest their salvation on the observance of a particular day.

A saloon-keeper in the town became interested in the meetings and was a constant attendant. One evening as we finished the hymn of invitation and the congregation had become seated, he stood like a statue, seemingly spellbound. I cried out to him, "Come forward and seek salvation, or else go home and write your name Satan on your signboard and come out in your true colors." He lived over his saloon. That night a fire caught in the saloon below, and suddenly awakened from sleep he thought the judgment had come. Springing from bed, he jumped out of the second story window, taking the sash with him. He began at once to seek salvation, but I believe did not make a very stable convert. Sister Himebaugh, afterwards Sister Updyke, who some time before had been miraculously healed by faith, was a great help in the meetings. Mother Lawrence was living at Geneva at the time, and by her prayers and faith helped immensely. Her husband greatly opposed and persecuted her and finally deserted her, and she got a divorce. She kept on her way, shouting amen as loud as ever, and after a few years her poor, old, former husband, broken down in health, came back and fell at her feet in humble confession. They were re-married; she helped him into the kingdom, and in a short time saw him safely off to heaven.

Quite a family by the name of Updyke were saved, and many additions were made to the class. One woman was clearly saved whose husband was greatly enraged. He burned her Bible, and when she undertook to pray would dash buckets of water on her. Finally he turned her outdoors. Mother Lawrence took her in, and we arranged to send her to Sister Coon's at Marengo. With his house desolate and himself thoroughly subdued, the man came to me and with tears besought me to tell him where he could find his wife. He very gladly paid my fare to accompany him to Marengo, and promising all that could be asked, his wife went home with him.

In the spring we set about building a church. Building stone was plentiful and cheap. I went out soliciting funds and met with quite a ready response. Brother Hackney, of Aurora, gave a hundred dollars, and others responded liberally and we felt warranted in beginning to build. I left the work before the house was completed. After I left they enlarged their plans and got so heavily in debt I believe the

property had to be sold. In all the years of my
ministry in our church this was the only circuit I
ever was appointed to which had not been raised up
under my own labors.

Camp-meetings were held year after year in
Brother Laughlin's grove. These meetings came to
be a kind of center from which radiated rays of
light, and from which influences of spiritual power
went out in all directions. The history of these
meetings has been graphically and faithfully written
by an abler pen than mine. I never can forget the
fearful onslaught made by the roughs one night
during the second meeting. The services of the
evening were over and all but a few on guard had
retired for rest, when suddenly the alarm was given
that the rowdies were tearing down tents. The
brethren rushed out and the rowdies fell back, but,
arming themselves with clubs and stakes, soon rallied
and came on for a general attack. Brother Terrill
took the lead of the camp-meeting forces and,
inspired with love for the cause of God and desire
for the safety of the campers, without fear, he
sallied out to meet the attacking forces, who, filled
with whisky, were yelling like demons from the
pit. Good Brother Newell Day, being acquainted
with some of the men, in the quietness and sweet-
ness of his spirit, went out to reason with them and

try and dissuade them from their murderous purpose. But in their insane frenzy they were beyond reasoning, and one of them, seizing a huge pointed stick, hurled it with all his might. The point of the missile struck Brother Day, gouging out one of his eyes. Groaning and crying out with pain Brother Day made his way back to the encampment. He was taken into a tent to be ministered to, and the brethren, rushing on the roughs, in almost a moment's time scattered them in all directions. They secured two or three of the ringleaders. They were brought before the magistrate and bound over for trial. But at that time the country was in a blaze of excitement on account of the Civil War, and to enlist was to cover a multitude of sins. These men enlisted and went off to the war. Some of them, at least, were known to have come to a miserable end.

Brother Day eventually went West and settled at Orleans, Nebraska, where he continued to live and walk with God until March 26, 1901, when he passed triumphantly to the better land.

At the session of the conference held at Clintonville in the fall of 1861 I was elected and ordained deacon. This was the session from which I was sent to St. Charles. At the session of the conference held at Aurora in the fall of 1862 Brother Roberts came to me and said he had received a

letter from a man in Michigan who wanted a Free
Methodist preacher sent to that State, and asked me
if I would go. I replied, "If you say so and I can
get there I will go to the North Pole." Before the
close of the session Brother Roberts said to me,
"We haven't men enough to supply the circuits, but
the brethren at Marengo have consented, if you are
sent there, to let you take three months at any time
of the year you may choose to visit Michigan."

Brother Roberts gave me the letter he had
received from Rev. H. L. Jones of Ida, Michigan,
and requested me to correspond with him and to
arrange if possible to go during the winter months,
as that would be the best time for holding revival
meetings.

We met with a very cordial reception from our
old friends at Marengo. We finished off the old
house at the rear of the church lot and had a very
comfortable parsonage. At the beginning of this
conference year our dear friend and spiritual father,
Rev. J. W. Redfield, was called to his eternal reward.
He had for more than two years suffered, at times
intensely, from a stroke of paralysis which had rendered one side almost completely helpless. He was
not able to preach, but would attend service and
give in his testimony. Osgood Joslyn, who was
saved in the first meeting the doctor held in Marengo,

took him to his home and cared for him while he lived. A few days before the doctor passed away he called Brother Joslyn to his bedside and said, " Osgood, I cannot live long, and I want you to take my last testimony and tell all the people for me that this is the track that leads to heaven."

In preaching the doctor had a peculiar way of bringing up and setting down his right foot, and at the same time with a good deal of emphasis shouting, Hallelujah! On the evening of his death, just as the breath left his body, in his characteristic way he brought up his foot and, as some who were looking on said, set it down in heaven. And so this good man passed on to his heavenly home. His body lies in the cemetery at Marengo, and on the stone at the head of the grave after the name and dates there is inscribed the single sentence: " He was true to his motto—Fidelity to God." Fortunately Brother Roberts had not returned East, and he was at once sent for to preach the funeral sermon. The services were held in our church at Marengo. The, day was very stormy, the rain falling in torrents, but the house was crowded. It was a solemn scene as the young preachers gathered around the casket to take the last look at that calm and heavenly face. Standing there with hands uplifted we sang the minister's prayer, hymn No. 298 of our present hymn book, and pledged ourselves anew to God. By a merciful providence the Lord had, as it were, taken the doctor from us by degrees, for during his two years' illness we had learned to look away from the arm of flesh and to trust more fully in God, so his death did not prove a shock or any great hindrance to the work.

By this time our Illinois conference began to assume respectable proportions. Cyrus Underwood was a shoe dealer in St. Louis. He was a professed infidel, but hearing of the doctor's meetings had the curiosity to hear the man. Whenever he went to church in those days he went to criticize. He seated himself in the church that evening, ready when the preacher should begin his sermon, to riddle it with the shot of criticism. But the young, would-be infidel was disarmed before the preacher reached the pulpit, for as the doctor in going up the aisle passed the pew in which Cyrus was sitting he was struck under conviction and at the first opportunity began to earnestly seek the Lord. He became a strong and successful preacher, but after some years of service became fearful as to the matter of support and went into secular business.

J. W. Dake became a Boanerges in the work, but not until, in the providence of God, he had been thrown out, under the Spirit, on his own resources.

At this session at Aurora the stationing committee were greatly perplexed over the appointment of J. W. Dake, and a committee was appointed to wait on him and advise him to locate. When the committee came to confer with Brother Dake, he said, "Very well, brethren, you take the responsibility of placing me in a local relation and I will gladly go back to my farm, but I don't dare request that relation." It was greater responsibility than the committee wished to assume, and as an old man had come up from Bureau county to ask for a preacher, Brother Dake, without a member or any assured support, was put down for Bureau county. Thrust out to sink or swim, he concluded by the grace and help of God not to sink, and came up the next year to report a swimming success. The only embarrassment the stationing committee ever had after that in the case of J. W. Dake was in trying to meet all the demands for his services.

Joseph Travis proved to be a successful laborer, and as a preacher he put his sermons together with about the same exactness with which he had formerly constructed railroad locomotives. N. D. Fanning was a highly educated young man, and naturally and easily preached sermons which would be a credit to a bishop. He was styled "The scholar of the Illinois conference." He finally went, I believe, to

the Presbyterians, and somewhere in Minnesota, I
understand, dropped dead in the pulpit while preaching one of his remarkable sermons. Thomas La Due
was pastor of the Congregational church at Saint
Charles. In the early days of our church in that
village he was gloriously saved, and preached holiness
so effectually that many of his members got the experience, and finally with him united with the Free
church. For several years he preached, both West
and East, with success, and from his quiet home near
Portland, Oregon, passed to take his place amid the
ransomed throng. He left two sons—men of studious
habits and sterling Christian character. The younger
one labored a few years in the California conference.
His praise was in all the churches. He died in holy
triumph. To this day by those who knew of him he
is remembered as the model preacher. The other
still lives, an efficient member of the faculty of
Greenville college. M. V. Clute came from Brother
La Due's church in Saint Charles, and, receiving
license to preach, was admitted to the traveling connection, and lived and died a member of the Illinois
conference.

But time would fail to appropriately speak of
Terrill and Mead and Cook and Harroun, of Bishop
and Shepardson and Ribble, and many others who
labored in the beginning of the work in the Illinois

conference.   At the session in the fall of 1862 some fifteen or twenty circuits, with a total membership of six or seven hundred were reported.

CHAPTER IX.

WE HAD expected, with perhaps the exception of a few weeks' labor in Michigan, to spend a pleasant and prosperous year in Marengo, but by the providence of God one quarter was destined to be the limit of our pastoral work in Illinois. During this quarter besides filling my regular appointments in Marengo I preached at several outside points. One Sabbath evening I was to be away, and secured, or supposed I had, the services of Brother C. E. Harroun for the church at Marengo. Judge of my surprise when on reaching home I found that Brother Harroun, although he had reached the place in time, instead of going into the church to preach had gone into the parsonage and remained during the service. I labored with him the best I could, calling his attention to that part of the Discipline which reads, "Be sure and never disappoint a congregation," when with all seriousness the brother replied, "Really, Brother Hart, I didn't know which would prove the greater disappointment to the congregation, to go in and try to preach or stay away."

The only special service we attempted to hold

was a watch-night meeting, but on New Year's eve there came on one of the worst storms ever experienced in Northern Illinois. On New Year's morning I dug out through the drifts and found by tracks in the snow that just one person had tried to reach the church door. I began correspondence with Rev. Mr. Jones, of Michigan, and arranged to be with him by January 24. When we started for Michigan our only child was about sixteen months old. We left her with my parents, who had both united with the Free church. My mother said she would gladly keep the child so that my wife might accompany me, "for," said she, "they that stay by the stuff share in the spoils with those who go to war "

Having given Brother Jones the date of our arrival, I expected him to meet us at Ida. Reaching Chicago I called at the office of the General Passenger Agent of the Michigan Southern railroad and requested clergy rates for myself and wife to Ida station. He informed me that it would be necessary to apply through the agent at Ida. I explained that I did not live at Ida, but desired rates there. He looked up, and in a mild but very firm tone said, "This is according to our rules, sir, and I have no discretion in the matter." I failed in getting rates, but out of the incident I got an illustration which at times I have been able to use to good advantage. It was this: The conditions of salvation are in such perfect accord with principles of right that we may as well meet them without questioning, for as far as making them any easier is concerned the Lord himself has no discretion.

Being of rather an imaginary turn of mind, I am quite given to forecasting and picturing out to myself coming events. So, as we journeyed along, I had our reception at Ida all thrown out on the canvas of imagination, and said to my wife, "When we reach Ida we shall be met by a decrepit old man with white hair, and with tobacco juice running down the corners of his beard. He will have an old gray horse and a broken-down buggy." On reaching Ida we found it to be a station and little else. There was a brick store and two or three dwellings. We had come from a prairie country and landed amid a forest of giant elms whose great branches stretched up toward the sky. The frozen black clay hubs stuck up through a light fall of snow, and to us the prospect was rather dreary. But to cap all, not even my old, white-haired, tobacco-stained man was there to meet us. We made our way to the store and inquired for Rev. Jones. The storekeeper gave us directions, and we started for a walk of a mile or more through the snow and over the hubs to find the residence of Brother Jones. I was carrying the grips and my wife had the lunch-basket. When we had covered about half the distance we set down the luggage for a rest, and turning to my wife I said, "Mat, this looks rather dubious, doesn't it?" Seizing the bail of the basket and starting, she began to sing, "While there's a track I'll never look back, but go on at the risk of my all."

This storekeeper was a German by the name of Rauch. At the time he was, I believe, a member of the Dutch Reformed church, but not many years after he got grandly saved and joined the Free Methodist church. To the day of his death he was one of our most reliable members. His wife survives him and for years has maintained a steady experience, continually realizing the blessing of the Lord. Some of their children have been a great help in the church. One daughter, now the wife of W. E. Bardell of the Illinois conference and manager of the Woodstock Orphanage and Home, has been especially efficient as a worker.

We finally came to a large, fine-looking farm-house, and upon knocking the door was opened by a pleasant-faced, elderly man. I inquired whether Rev. H. L. Jones lived there. He replied, "No, sir," and pointing to a house across the fields said, "He lives over there," and then added, "He is not at home, but I am his father." I said, "My name is

Hart. I am a Free Methodist preacher from Illinois. I have been corresponding with your son"—and before I could say more the old gentleman grasped my hand and cried out, "God bless you, Brother and Sister Hart. Come in! Come in!" Father Jones informed us that his son had gone up to a point on the Macon river, called East Milan, to arrange for a quarterly meeting, and that he was to take us up there the next morning.

And now let us notice the providence by which the way was opened for our work in Michigan. Some years prior to our arrival in the State Father Jones and others, members of the Methodist Episcopal church, deploring the lack of spirituality, decided to organize a new denomination, which they called The Methodist Episcopal Conformist Church —the word "Conformist" being expressive of their determination to conform to the doctrines and Discipline of primitive Methodism. For a few years they met with success and at one time in Southeastern Michigan numbered some three or four hundred. But in every truly evangelical movement history repeats itself, and this little branch was soon called to encounter very bitter worldly and Satanic opposition, so that at the time of our advent into the State their membership was sadly diminished and Henry Jones was the only remaining preacher.

A Free Methodist woman from Buffalo, New York, went to Michigan to visit her sister, a Mrs. Knoll, who was a member of the Conformist church. The sister from Buffalo had a copy of the *Earnest Christian*, which at that time Brother Roberts was publishing in that city. Sister Knoll handed the periodical to Henry Jones, who read it carefully and then wrote Brother Roberts for a copy of the Discipline. Having studied this with care he wrote Brother Roberts, requesting him to send them a Free Methodist preacher. So in this instance, as in many others, the *Earnest Christian* proved to be a John the Baptist and forerunner for our work. And from this beginning six or seven annual conferences, with two or three hundred traveling preachers and a membership of over six thousand, have been added to our Zion. Surely this periodical has some claim on our people for support.

The next morning after our arrival Father Jones by private conveyance took us some twelve miles to East Milan, where Henry Jones had arranged for a quarterly meeting. The services were held in a fine, large schoolhouse. Near by was the residence of Shubal Lewis, where we were entertained. Brother Lewis was a member of the Methodist Episcopal church, but his wife belonged with the Conformists. Brother Lewis was a thrifty farmer. Sister Lewis was a woman whose very countenance conveyed the impression of intelligent devotion to principle.

Our meeting on Saturday afternoon was well attended and characterized by a good degree of the Spirit's presence. At the close of the service I called together the members of the Conformist church who were present, read from our Discipline and made known to them as clearly as I could the origin and aim of the Free Methodist church. They seemed greatly pleased with us and our representation of our people; so much so that I thought it necessary to inform them that as a church we had our trials, and that it was not always smooth sailing with us. But they were so favorably impressed that they decided to invite us to remain and hold meetings at different points, and, if in my judgment I thought best, to organize societies and lay the foundation for Free Methodism in Michigan. Fanaticism and jealousy had sadly divided and destroyed the work, but the self-seeking and reckless element had withdrawn, and the few who were left were as candid and as intelligently religious as any company of people with whom it has ever been my privilege to labor.

On Sabbath the place was thronged and the Lord came in power. At the close of the preaching, preparatory to administering the sacrament, I read and

explained the general directions and invitation of
the Discipline. Sister Lewis up to this time had
dressed in plain and modest attire, but had finally
yielded to the entreaties of her family, and on this
Sunday morning came out with a new bonnet
trimmed with artificial flowers. While I was reading
and explaining the Discipline I noticed the large
tear-drops coursing down the good woman's cheeks,
and as the invitation to the communion was given
she deliberately laid off her bonnet, and, drawing
her veil over her head, came forward and partook of
the emblems of the body and blood of the crucified
Savior. This act on the part of this intelligent and
highly respected Christian woman made a deep and
lasting impression on the minds of the people in that
community. Some months after I received this
noble woman into the church, where she remained a
staunch member to the day of her death. In uniting
with the church she acted with the same calm, delib-
erate determination that characterized her course in
the communion service of our first Sabbath in Michigan. Years after, when some little friction arose in
the society, some one suggested that she better leave
the class. "Oh, no!" she replied, "I know too well
what it cost me to join. It was the Free Methodist
church or hell with me."

We closed our meeting at East Milan with our

Sabbath evening service, and returning with Father Jones, held meetings for a few evenings in the schoolhouse in his neighborhood. Here we met quite a remarkable character, known throughout all that region by the cognomen of "Happy Jimmy." All the former part of his life had been spent on the ocean as a sailor before the mast. Several years before the time of which I write he came into Monroe county, and by working as a farm hand just managed to live. He had professed religion for several years, but every time he went to Monroe, the county seat, he was sure to get drunk. He would be very penitent, and the people in their pity for him would forgive him. This was repeated over and over until finally Jimmy, determined on victory or death, went out into an orchard and for a day and a night, as I have frequently heard him say (but people who were acquainted with the case said that it was two days and two nights), wrestled under the apple tree; and that proved to be the Waterloo for the drink habit with Jimmy. He never got drunk again. Ever after he was enabled to give a clear testimony to the power of Jesus' blood to cleanse from all sin.

When I became acquainted with Jimmy he was an old man, living in the family of a good widow, who kindly cared for him till the day of his death. Although Jimmy could not read, he was perfectly familiar with the Bible, as he also was with the biographies of all the early Methodist saints, frequently quoting from Wesley, Fletcher, Bramwell and others. He was quite diminutive in stature, and, as he depended on the charity of the people for his wardrobe, he sometimes made quite a ludicrous appearance—his coat large enough perhaps to wrap twice around him, and a leather strap around his loins, with a high silk hat which someone had discarded and which was two or three sizes too large for him, with an old rag stuffed up in front to keep the hat in place on his head, he certainly made a very grotesque appearance. But the few who are living who in those days knew "Happy Jimmy," and whose eyes may fall on these lines, will recall with gladness the trite and pithy testimonies of that remarkable man of God. At one time, in speaking of walking several miles one bitter cold day in winter to attend a meeting, he said, " I thought for a while I should perish, but I got down on my knees in the snow and prayed and straightly the cold obated." On one occasion he was relating to a preacher some wonderful manifestation he had witnessed under the power of God, when the preacher exclaimed, "I don't believe a word of it." "Well, then," said Jimmy, "that makes you out an unbeliever." In some meetings Jimmy's shouts of praise were too much for refined ears, and so when he got

full to overflowing he would break for the door and
do his shouting outside.

At first when Jimmy came to our meeting as the
tide reached a certain point he would give a whoop
and rush out. Finally Sister Hart asked him why
he went out. "Oh," he replied, "I don't want to dis-
turb the meeting." Sister Hart assured him it was
no disturbance to praise God in our meeting, and
that Brother Hart would rather have him stay and
praise the Lord in the house. After that in our services we had the benefit of the overflow of this
chosen vessel of the Lord. In testifying he would
usually start up suddenly and speak a few words and
sit down. At one time I remember his testimony
was about as follows: "I am all glorious within. My
soul is like the king's daughter—it is all hung with
jewels." One morning they went up to his room to
call him for breakfast, and, getting no response, entered his room and found him lying as though he
were quietly sleeping; but it proved to be the sleep
of death. Some time during the night he had passed
away, evidently without a struggle. "He lived happy,
and died happy, and was saved. Be not surprised.
He loved and served his God."

CHAPTER X.

THE only church building owned by the Conformists was at a place called Otter Creek. This was on the old plank road running from Monroe to Toledo. The house had not been used for some time, and there was some question as to the validity of the title. The brethren thought we had better go to Otter Creek and hold some meetings, and if possible resurrect the work there and secure the church property. There was one member, a Brother A., who owned and operated a saw-mill, still living there. Father Jones furnished us with a horse and buggy, and arranged for a boy to go down and take the conveyance back. We were instructed to go to the house of this Brother A. for entertainment. Reaching the place about noon we found the house of the brother. I knocked at the door and told the woman who answered the summons who we were, and that we had come to hold some meetings in the church, and that Father Jones had directed us to their house. Speaking up quite tartly she said, "If you want to see Mr. A. you will find him at the mill," and shut the door in my face.

Going out to the buggy I said to my wife, "Mat, we have money enough to pay our way at a tavern for a day or two, and we will stop awhile, anyway." Driving around to the tavern—a drinking place on the old plank, it could hardly be called a hotel—I told the man to feed the horse and that a boy would soon call for it, and that we wanted accommodations for a day or so. After dinner we hunted up the key to the church, went to the schoolhouse and gave notice of the meeting for the evening. We then started out to call from house to house, to talk and pray with the people. To our surprise we found that but comparatively few of them could understand English, being mostly Lutherans or German Catholics.

A small congregation gathered in the evening, and we preached and exhorted them the best we could. In the morning, breakfast over, I told the landlord that we usually had family prayers where we stopped, and asked him if he had any objection to our having worship in the sitting-room. "Oh, no," he replied. I requested him to call in his family, and he called his wife, all the family he had. We read and sang and prayed with them. I talked with him about selling liquor. He said he knew it was wrong, but added, "I have to live." The old lady was visibly affected, and on questioning her we found she was an old once-in-grace-always-in-grace Baptist backslider. The poor old woman with pipe in mouth would follow Sister Hart around and sob and cry like a child. In a day or so someone invited us to stop with him, and I told our landlord I would pay our bill. He quickly replied, "Not a cent, sir; not a cent, and if you ever come this way again make our house your home." By Sabbath Brother A. ventured to invite us to dinner. We found Mrs. A. very much modified in her attitude towards us, and had a very pleasant time with them. As Otter Creek did not prove to be a very promising field, we returned to the Ida neighborhood.

One day as I was riding with Henry Jones on the old plank between Monroe and Adrian we passed a large farmhouse bearing the appearance of having at one time been a country hotel. As we drove by the place Brother Jones remarked, "If the man living here should get saved it would stir this whole country." On inquiry I learned that his name was John Plues. When we started for Otter Creek Henry Jones said, "I will go and begin a meeting in the Plues schoolhouse, and if there proves to be a good interest you can come later." On our return to Ida we found that Henry had been holding a meeting in the Plues schoolhouse about one week. We had been away from home now some four weeks or more.

We had left a fine charge in a beautiful village, with a church and parsonage on the same lot, with surroundings about all one could wish. And above all our only child, just at that age when children with their innocent prattle begin to be the most interesting, was at home and we were getting homesick and anxious to return to our charge. So as we went to the Plues neighborhood that afternoon I had decided that unless there should prove to be unusual indications for good this would be our last attempt in trying to raise up a work in Michigan, and that we should shortly return home. With this determination in mind, as we went to the schoolhouse that evening I said to my wife, "Mat, to-night it is either make or break."

In my experience in holding revival meetings I have never seen a deep and thorough work of saving grace among the people until I have been brought to keenly realize my utter inability to accomplish anything. Not until, in fact, on the very ragged edge of despair I have been brought to realize and to cry, "When my all of strength shall fail I shall with the God-man prevail." When brought to know my own utter helplessness, and halting on the shrunken thigh of my own endeavor I have been forced to cry, "Yield to me now, for I am weak; but confident in self-despair," then it is that God comes to speak

PLATE 5. SCHOOLHOUSE.

blessing to my soul, and is conquered by my instant prayer.

By this time "the new preacher and his wife from Illinois" had become quite a theme of conversation, and at our first service at the Plues schoolhouse we were greeted by a large congregation. We were both deeply burdened for the work, and felt it was time for the power of God to come on the people. In the opening prayer Sister Hart reached the throne, and in the earnestness of intercession literally screamed in agony for the Lord to come. For a text I took the last part of the third verse of the third chapter of Matthew: "Prepare ye the way of the Lord, make his paths straight." The Spirit enabled me to emphasize the fact that as the Lord was to come to the Jews of old. either in salvation or in damnation, so he would come to each one of us, and that the command to prepare his way referred not to the fact but to the manner of his coming. The people listened with breathless attention, and many were deeply convicted. When I gave an invitation for seekers, quite a number responded, among them the wife and twin daughters, two beautiful girls of about seventeen, and one or two younger children of John Plues. There were remarkable manifestations of divine power in the altar service and several professed salvation.

As we were about to close I told Brother Jones I thought it would be well to have some afternoon meetings at private houses. He spoke of my suggestion and inquired if anyone would open his house for an afternoon meeting. As no one responded, Brother Jones spoke to a tall man sitting on a desk about midway in the house, and said, "Mr. Plues, can we have a meeting at your house to-morrow afternoon?" Rather gruffly Mr. Plues answered, "I don't care." So the meeting for the following afternoon was announced to be at the house of John Plues.

A day or so before this the youngest son of Father Jones had died, and at the hour of the afternoon meeting at the house of Mr. Plues I was to attend the funeral services. As Henry Jones would be one of the mourners, I said to my wife, "You must lead the meeting at Mr. Plues' while I go to attend the funeral." Plues had for some time been engaged in splitting rails, but on the afternoon of the meeting decided he would not go out to split rails but stay and attend, for, as he afterwards told us, he thought if he went to the woods we would think he was afraid. Sister Hart led the meeting, exhorting the people to seek salvation. Meanwhile John Plues was sitting and staring at her with a bold, derisive look. At the close of the service Mr. Plues went out and took a seat by the fireplace in the kitchen.

Sister Hart, that she might come in closer contact with the sneering scoffer, took occasion to go out at the kitchen door, and as she passed Mr. Plues she inquired, "Do you enjoy religion?" He answered gruffly, "I don't know but I do." Looking at him solemnly Sister Hart then inquired, "Are you ready for death and the judgment?" A little cowed, and as he afterwards told us, "I thought I had lied to the woman once and I wouldn't lie again," he rather meekly replied, "I don't know that I am." "Well," said Sister Hart, "I warn you to get ready for death and the judgment," and passed on.

John Plues was a man of strong personality. Tall, lank and bony, standing six feet four in his stocking feet. In his general appearance he reminded me strongly of the pictures of Abraham Lincoln. He was descended from an aristocratic English family. He inherited quite a tract of land, but, not being much of a farmer, accumulating indebtedness was gradually eating away his estate. For some years he had run a hotel, but on the advent of the railroad, some miles to the south, travel was diverted from the old plank road and hotel keeping did not pay. Mr. Plues built a long ballroom on to his house, and several times each year would advertise a dance, and as his wife was a fine cook these gatherings became quite popular.

At the meeting at the schoolhouse the next evening Mrs. Plues and her daughters were forward again
and began to get out into the light. When they
reached home at the close of the meeting that evening Mrs. Plues said to her husband, "John, I want to
ask your forgiveness for any wrong I have ever done,
and I would like to read the Bible and pray before
we retire." In an angry tone he replied, "I'll never
forgive you, and there shall be no reading the Bible
and praying in my house;" and then added, "These
preachers are not coming here to tell my family
what to do. How do you know who this couple
from Illinois are? Probably just off some theater
boards! Why," said he, "I saw him give that woman
the wink and she knew just what to do." The wife
breathed her heart out in silent prayer to God and
then retired. But John could not sleep. He thought
how mean he had been to his wife. She had asked
his forgiveness and he would not forgive her. She
wanted to read the Bible and pray with her family
and he would not allow that. He rolled restlessly
on the bed, and finally, the agony becoming too
intense to be borne, thoroughly subdued, he spoke
up and said, "Samantha, do you think those preachers
would come and pray for me?" Quick as thought
the wife replied, "Why, yes, John, and I'll pray for
you too." So up they got and went to praying. We

were stopping with a Methodist family by the name
of G. The farms of John Plues and this Timothy G.
joined, and for a long time ill will had existed
between them.

About daylight Mrs. Plues in breathless haste
knocked at the door of Timothy G. and said, "Oh,
John is praying and he wants the preachers to come
and pray for him," and added, "he wants you to
come, too, Timothy." We could see that this was
a choker for Timothy, but there was no other way;
and breakfast and family prayers over, out we started.
Henry Jones and wife, my wife and myself, Timothy and wife and their daughter who was seeking,
all made our way over to see the seeking penitent.
I was then in my twenty-ninth year and weighed
about one hundred and thirty pounds. As we entered
the house we found Mr. Plues bowed under the
weight of grief that was upon him, his eyes inflamed
and swollen from weeping, and he was dressed in a
short, ragged coat which, in his haste, he had drawn
on. He certainly was a pitiful looking object. As
I led the way into the room Plues caught me up in
his arms, raising me completely from the floor, and
in the most beseeching tone cried out, "O Mr. Hart,
am I in the strait way? Am I in the strait way?"
"Well," I replied, "you look like it, but let us pray."
We held on to God till the man was clearly con-

verted; until peace, consciously realized by nearly everyone in the room, came to his soul. Before Brother Plues arose from his knees he began to cry, "O my neighbors! my neighbors! We must go and see my neighbors." Getting up from prayer he went straight to Mr. G., and grasping his hand cried out, "O Timothy, how we have lived! how we have lived!" Timothy, breaking down, confessed up and the enmity of these men whose farms joined was gone.

The conversion of John Plues was a very important link in the chain of providences by which our work was established in Michigan. As the sequel will show it was the key to the train of providences by which thousands were brought to a saving knowledge of the truth. For years, as the calls for work increased and doors were continually opening, I felt and repeatedly gave expression to the thought that Michigan seemed like a ripe pear which must speedily be plucked or it would be lost to our work. And I presume that to-day two or three miles outside the beaten track of our old circuits, almost anywhere, effectual open doors may still be found.

A dozen or fifteen of us started out from the Plues residence to visit and pray with the neighbors, John Plues and myself leading the procession. The first call was at the house of Mr. Clark. As we entered we found Mrs. Clark skimming milk. Mr.

Clark made no profession of religion; his wife claimed to be a Presbyterian. They were greatly surprised as they saw us marching up the walk towards their house and at once concluded that something unusual had transpired. As we walked in and took seats Mrs. Clark was greatly agitated. She tried to keep at her work but was so excited she could accomplish nothing. Brother Plues began at once to tell what God had done for him, when Mrs. Clark cried out excitedly, "Mr. Plues, you are excited. How do we know who these people are?" Then she went on with a great story about a temperance lecturer who had been through there and turned out badly. Brother Plues was taken aback for it was evident that he supposed everybody would at once break down and set about seeking religion. I looked at the woman and quietly remarked, "Madam, if I should prove to be the devil you need salvation, don't you?"

To John Plues the case seemed an urgent one and he exclaimed, "Mr. Hart, you pray. Mrs. Hart, you shout." By shouting Plues referred to the first night of our meeting at the schoolhouse when, as he afterwards told us, every scream uttered by Sister Hart in prayer went like a dagger to his soul. Mr. Clark was deeply convicted but seemed to stand in fear of his wife. After prayer with these people we passed on to the house of Mr. Brown. The father and boys seeing such a crowd coming up the road ran to the barn. Mrs. Brown broke down and was saved on the spot. Mrs. Brown falling into line we went on to the house of James Galloway. He and his wife both earnestly sought and came out very clearly saved. We went on from house to house, the people with few exceptions breaking down and crying for mercy. That night the schoolhouse was altogether too small to accommodate the crowd which gathered. The meeting became an assured success. Brother Plues said, "The people do not come out to see John the Baptist but John the sinner." He had a great desire to see his neighbor G. clearly saved. He would say to him, "Timothy, we must confess." "Oh," said Timothy, "I did confess at the beginning of the meeting." "O yes," says John, "but new people are coming out and we must confess every night."

We improvised seats and converted Plues' ball-room into a house of prayer, holding afternoon meetings in it every day. Brother Plues took his Bible and visited the people for miles in every direction. Some seventy-five or a hundred were converted, and it began to look as though salvation under the auspices of the Free Methodist church had come to Michigan to stay.

After the conversion of John Plues we were entertained at his house until our departure for Illinois. Brother Plues began to read and study the Bible, for up to this time he had hardly ever looked into it, and for a man of his general intelligence was remarkably deficient in the knowledge of its contents. Quite a number of laborers, some of whom afterwards became efficient ministers of the New Testament, were brought out in this meeting. One bright boy of about fourteen was saved, and in passing out of meeting one day I laid my hand on his head and said, "Bub, I think the Lord has a work for you to do." Three or four years later he was licensed to preach and for some thirty or more years Ellsworth Leonardson has been doing efficient service for the Master. He labored several years in Michigan and Ohio, afterwards in Kansas, and is now a district elder in the Southern California conference. An older brother, who a short time before this had been converted, one day in company with his brother-in-law came to me and with considerable embarrassment made known the fact that they felt called to preach the gospel. I gave them some words of encouragement and they were soon out calling sinners to repentance. The brother-in-law finally went to the Congregationalists but the brother is still with us and at this writing is pastor of our church at Cleveland, Ohio.

This series of meetings continued for a month or more, and I began to be quite anxious to get home. One day as my wife and I were talking about our plans for the future I told her I thought I should advise these converts to join some church and be sure and live religion, and we would go back to Illinois and would meet them in heaven. Just then Brother Plues came into the room and said, "Brother Hart, what are you going to do with us people?" I told him that my wife and I were just talking the matter over and repeated what I had said to Sister Hart. Turning to me with a kind of a leer in his eyes he said, "No, s-i-r; you have got us into this boat and you must see us through." I quickly responded, "By the grace of God we will, Brother Plues." I at once wrote Brother Roberts and he replied, "Stay, by all means."

Arranging for Henry Jones to keep up the appointments we returned to Marengo, Illinois, and made known our determination to go back and remain in Michigan. For the few weeks we were in Marengo packing up for Michigan we were continually beset by objectors and objections. My wife would pull up carpets and pack with the tears running, and good brethren and sisters very emphatically declaring that our going was all of the wicked one, and that we were running from the burden, etc.

Here we were with a nice new church building, a comfortable parsonage, parents, together with uncles and aunts on both sides and with many others who were about as dear to us, and were preparing to go where we would have no certain dwelling place and no visible means of support, liable at any time to a charge of vagrancy.

We told the people that we had authority from Brother Roberts for our course, but this availed nothing. Some said, "If a conference should be raised up in Michigan we would not believe your going was of the Lord." Letters were sent on to Brother Roberts, and years afterwards he laughingly said to us, "I don't know when I have been abused as I was for consenting to your going to Michigan." Feeling, however, that the Lord so directed, we persisted in our course.

Brother C. S. Gitchell, a young student from Garrett Biblical Institute, was engaged to supply the work, and amid the tears and protests of our friends we left Marengo for our new field in Michigan. Brother Gitchell under the circumstances did remarkably well. He labored two years or so in Illinois, then went over to Michigan, and proved to be one of our most efficient workers, his special forte being the raising up of new circuits and building churches. The work was greatly strengthened and built up in Michigan, Ohio and Indiana through his labors. Laid aside from active work, he is now a member of the North Michigan conference.

CHAPTER XI.

ON OUR return trip to Michigan, at the request of C. S. Gitchell, we stopped at Mishawaka, Indiana, and visited his father who was a local preacher in the Methodist Episcopal church. I preached one evening and went on to Osseo, Hillsdale county, Michigan. I had been requested to preach at the Black schoolhouse, as it was called, about four miles south of Osseo. A man by the name of Van Orman had agreed to meet us at Osseo. He had instructed me to go to the store at the station and wait for him. Our child was taken quite sick on the train and when we reached Osseo was very ill and threatened with spasms. We went to the store as directed and after waiting several hours I concluded I would walk down to the neighborhood where I expected to preach and send back a conveyance for my wife and baby. I found the house of Mr. Van Orman, and knocking at the door his wife made her appearance. I told her who I was and the object of my call. In very positive tones she informed me that her husband and the team were busy in the field and could not be spared to go to the station. So I trudged back through the heat and dust and found that the store-keeper had kindly invited Sister Hart to go into his house adjoining the store.

We were in something of a dilemma, having just about money enough to pay our fare to Ida, but not enough for hotel bill and fare. We concluded to go to the hotel for the night and trust in the Lord to help us through. As we were getting ready to start out the merchant's wife invited us to stop to supper. We gladly accepted the invitation, and learning that they were members of the Methodist church I inquired the name of their preacher, and found it was Van Antwerp. Sister Hart quickly inquired, "Is his wife's name Jennie?" The lady answered, "It is." Before their marriage we had known Brother and Sister Van Antwerp. They were both saved in one of Doctor Redfield's meetings in Illinois. Sister Hart lost no time in making her way to the parsonage. She was cordially received, and on explaining our circumstances Brother Van Antwerp said, "Go and tell Brother Hart to come right home." Reaching the house of the kind-hearted minister, his wife prepared some simple remedy, and our baby was soon much better. We thanked the Lord and took courage. The following day we made our way to Ida where we found Brother Plues waiting to welcome us and take us to his house. I had an appointment out for a quarterly meeting for the following Sabbath. "And the same time there arose no small stir about that way," and a large crowd was expected to be in attendance.

Previous to our return to Illinois, perhaps about the fourteenth of February, Sister Hart received a valentine in the shape of an article clipped from some denominational paper concerning the special duties of preachers' wives and asserting that they had none, but they, like other women, were called to remain at home and care for their families, and closed up with the inquiry, "While you are out preaching to the heathen abroad who is caring for your little heathen at home?" As Sister Hart read the paper she exclaimed, "I pray the Lord to bless the person who sent this with conviction," and as the sequel shows the prayer was answered. In the neighborhood adjoining that of the Lewis school-house was an old Baptist church building. The society kept together, but had no regular preaching. Lemuel T. Frink was one of the deacons and a leading man in this church. Mr. Frink worked his farm summers, and, being a well educated man, taught school during the winter. Mrs. Frink was not only intelligent but a woman of remarkable resolution as well, and if a failure to heartily endorse the doctrine of predestination constitutes a reprobate she cer-

tainly was one. This lady had attended some of our
meetings and in company with Sister Lewis came to
the quarterly meeting mentioned above. They were
entertained at the home of Brother Plues where we
stopped. We had frequently spoken to Sister Lewis
about our baby and now I took the child into the
sitting-room to show her to Sister Lewis. As I did
so I laughingly said, "All I care about that valentine
we received is that they called my baby a heathen."
Mrs. Frink was a stranger to us and we had no
thought that she knew anything about what I
referred to, but she had sent the clipping from the
paper. She said nothing at that time, but a few
months later at a grove-meeting held in Father
Jones' neighborhood, just as we were about to leave
for Illinois to attend the conference, she began to
earnestly seek the Lord. She struggled and prayed
for awhile, but did not get through. Finally taking
Sister Hart and myself one side, amid sobs and tears
she said, "Oh! would you believe that I could have
been so mean as to send you that valentine? Oh!
can you forgive me?" "O yes," said Sister Hart.
"I prayed the Lord to send conviction to the one
who sent it and he has answered my prayer. Praise
his name." "Oh!" said Mrs. Frink, "when Brother
Hart at the quarterly meeting brought in his baby
and spoke as he did to Sister Lewis I thought, Oh,

if I could only fall through the floor." All was for-
given and the good woman got blessed in her soul.

At the quarterly meeting I arranged to hold a
grove-meeting in the Plues neighborhood to commence June 13, and as Brother Roberts on his way
to meetings in Illinois was about this time to pass
through Michigan, I arranged with him to stop and
attend this meeting. During the few weeks intervening between the quarterly meeting and the grove-
meeting I traveled all over that section, preaching
and advertising the basket-meeting, calling especial
attention to the fact that Rev. B. T. Roberts, our
general superintendent, was to be present. The report of "this new kind of religion," as it was called,
had gone out in all directions, and when the time for
the meeting arrived people drove in for miles to see
and to hear. From Hillsdale county, some seventy
miles west of us, came quite a motley crowd. The
leading spirits among them were an old Englishman
and his daughter Elizabeth. With them were several persons, one of whom claimed to be a preacher.
The daughter Helizabeth, as the old gentleman persisted in calling her, also claimed to have a call to
preach, and on several occasions had attempted to
respond to the call. These people had heard of the
Free Methodists, and evidently supposed that noise
and demonstrations were the surest passports to

favor among them. In going from the house where
they were entertained to the grove they had so much
religion they would fall in the road and shout at the
top of their voices. We did not attempt to put any
straps on them, but accorded them the largest liberty.

On Saturday morning I sent a team to Monroe
City to meet Brother Roberts and convey him to the
meeting. Judge of my disappointment when on his
return the man informed me that Brother Roberts
had not come. I had done the preaching so far, and
decided on Saturday afternoon to put up the man of
the Hillsdale party who claimed to be a preacher.
A large congregation assembled, and all in eager
expectation of hearing our bishop. Uncouth in appearance, in manner and in phrase, the preacher announced his text and for an hour or so harangued us
in a style which would hardly be classed under the
head of either the hortatory, argumentative or ana-
lytical. Sister Hart retired behind a tree. I stood
my ground, taxing my mind as to the best method
of bringing order out of confusion. The speaker
gave us to distinctly understand that he had not
come from college halls. A large proportion of the
congregation supposed that they were listening to
the bishop, and were evidently greatly disappointed.

As soon as the brother brought his effort to a
close I sprang to my feet and announced that Brother

Roberts had not arrived, but that we hoped to have him for the Sabbath morning service.

I preached Saturday evening, and on retiring that night earnestly prayed that Brother Roberts might put in an appearance by morning. Sabbath morning the sun came up bright and clear, and in the freshness of early summer that grove of beech and maples seemed almost like a paradise. With one exception everything seemed favorable for success in the services of the day. Brother Roberts had not arrived. Giving the love-feast into the hands of Henry Jones, I made my way to Plues' ballroom and looked to the Lord for help to preach. These words, "Blessed are they which do hunger and thirst after righteousness for they shall be filled" (Matt. 5: 6), were impressed on my heart and mind. The hour for preaching had about arrived. A was walking back and forth in the ballroom, trying to get the line of thought fixed in my mind, when suddenly John Plues came bounding into the room shouting, "Glory be to God, Roberts has come!" Breathing a sigh of relief, as fast as my feet could carry me I made my way to the grove and greeted Brother Roberts. I allowed the love-feast to run for a little, and turning to Brother Roberts told him it was time for preaching. To my utter astonishment Brother Roberts replied, "I am not going to preach;

you will have to do the preaching this morning."
Finding him fixed in his determination, I went at it
and did the best I could. Brother Roberts followed
with a powerful exhortation, and salvation came.
Brother Roberts preached in the afternoon with
great liberty, and the people went away well satisfied
with our bishop. As many had come from a long
distance, we had no meeting at night. It seems that
on his way Brother Roberts had been detained in
Canada and did not reach Ida station until late Saturday night, and Father Jones brought him over
Sunday morning (see pages 346, 347, Life of Roberts).

All through the grove-meeting the company from
Hillsdale county were quite anxious to join the
church and be authorized to raise up classes in the
section where they lived, but not being very favorably impressed with their appearance, I put them off.
When Brother Roberts arrived they renewed their
application and urged him to receive them and au-
thorize them to hold meetings and organize classes.
Finally, as they were pressing their case with Brother
Roberts, I interfered, and partly as a protection to
Brother Roberts, said, "I have charge of this work,
and you will be obliged to consult with me." Brother
Roberts looked up from his reading and said, "You
will have to arrange with Brother Hart with refer-

ence to the work here." I told them I intended to go on to Illinois with Brother Roberts to attend the Saint Charles camp-meeting, and that I would stop at their place on my way back and spend a Sabbath with them, and if I thought best would then organize them into a class.

Sister Hart remained to help in the work, and I went on with Brother Roberts to attend the camp-meeting. I visited the friends at Marengo. Brother C. S. Gitchell was preaching there, and at that time they had a membership of over one hundred. The camp-meeting at Saint Charles was largely attended and one of the best ever held on that ground. On my return trip to Ida I stopped off at Hillsdale and spent the Sabbath with the people who attended our grove-meeting and who were so anxious to join the church. My fears as to their eligibility were confirmed, and I told them plainly I could not organize them into a class. The old gentleman said his daughter had appointments in the southern part of Hillsdale county, and urged me to form a circuit and appoint the girl as preacher in charge. This young woman not only was unable to read, but boasted of her ignorance and publicly proclaimed that seeing she was so ignorant her pulpit efforts must be all of the Lord. I gave them to understand that at some future time I might, in company with my wife, make them a visit. Going on to Monroe county, I planned a campaign for the summer. Living on the Rasin river, some four miles below the Plues schoolhouse, was a family by the name of Atkinson, who were Quakers. Years before the father and mother and six or seven sons had come from New Jersey and settled in the township of Raisinville. Most of the sons had families and places of their own, but Jonathan, the youngest, and his wife Carrie lived on the old homestead and cared for the parents. Jonathan and wife were members of the Conformist church, but soon united with our people, and while they lived were prominent among the laity of the church.

We were now having calls from every direction, and getting the loan of a buggy and harness from Brother Plues and a horse from Brother Atkinson we started to spy out the land. We went from neighborhood to neighborhood, preaching in a different schoolhouse each night. This was kept up nearly all of the remainder of the summer, sometimes not being able to commence services until nearly nine o'clock. Oftentimes the schoolhouse would be crowded and as many more standing outside, so taking my position in the door I would announce my text and preach to those outside as well as inside the house. In this way our work became thoroughly advertized throughout all that part of the State. This

was at the time of the Civil war, when the resources
of the country were being taxed to the uttermost.
Money was scarce and all the necessities of life com-
manded high prices, the most ordinary cotton prints
being fifty cents per yard. But we were welcomed
to the homes of the people, and without missionary
appropriation or aid saw the work of the Lord move
on in power.

We received a letter from the man in Hillsdale
county, urging us to come and go with them on
their round of appointments in the southern part of
the county. I wrote him that I could not go at
present as I did not have the money for railroad fare.
Not many days passed before I received another
communication from the man, with five dollars
enclosed. We went to what we called the Wilkerson schoolhouse, intending to hold a series of meetings. Brother and Sister Wilkerson were old and
tried saints, and when in that vicinity we always
made their house our home. We were considerably
perplexed as to the right course to pursue with
reference to the call from Hillsdale county. We
finally concluded we would return the five dollars
and inform the man that we could not go there. I
wrote the letter, enclosing the money, and my wife
and I started for a drive of several miles over the
old plank road to get to a postoffice to mail the

letter. The road was rough, our minds were not fairly settled, and we had quite a peculiar experience in trying to reach the office, for although no speaking ass stood in our way, a clear conviction came to both of us that we were going contrary to the will of God in refusing to go to Hillsdale, so finally we turned back, concluding to comply with the old gentleman's request. We wrote him to that effect and gave him the date on which to meet us at Hillsdale station. We returned to Brother Plues' house and found a letter from home stating that Sister Coon was to pass through Michigan on her way East, and if we desired would stop a few days with us. We wrote back, giving the date of our visit to Hillsdale, and requested her to meet us there.

Leaving our baby with the Plues girls we went on to Hillsdale, where Sister Coon met us. We waited at the hotel until the old gentleman and wife and daughter came along in a heavy farm wagon to take us to Steamburg, about four miles south, where the girl had an appointment for that Saturday evening. On the way the young woman told us of her wonderful efforts in preaching the gospel, until Sister Coon could stand it no longer and said to her, "My dear girl, stop talking about preaching; but if the Lord enables you to do any little thing for him do it and say nothing about it." I made some inquiries about the people in the neighborhood where we were going and the girl said, "Oh, they are an ignorant set!" "Why," said she, "the last time I was there and gave out the appointment we are going to, a young man at the close of the meeting came up and inquired how much the admittance would be the next time I came. I said, 'It will be nothing; this is a free gospel.' 'Oh,' he said, 'I thought it would be a quarter at least.'" I began to mistrust that the people had more intelligence than the girl gave them credit for, and that they were ridiculing her. Arriving at the place we found a large steam mill, from which the corners derived its name. It was in the midst of a rich farming country. The schoolhouse was a large frame building having a belfry and a bell. As it was about time for meeting we drove directly to the schoolhouse. I could see that the people had been drawn together largely by curiosity, and there seemed to be anything but a spirit of devotion there. There was no light in the house. After a little the old gentleman came to me and said it was time for preaching. I confess that I felt a little like keeping in the background, and said to him, "The people have come out to hear your daughter and probably she had better preach." He went to tell her to preach when some one in the vestibule asked him if there was not a Free Methodist preacher present. He said there was, when the person replied, "We can hear your daughter at some other time; we want to hear him to-night." The father came back and told me that some Wesleyan Methodists were there and wanted to hear a Free Methodist preach. I felt that I had made a mistake, so said at once, "Ill preach."

Stepping up behind the desk I inquired, "Can we have a light?" Several persons went out and brought in lamps, and now curiosity was at a higher pitch than before. We began to sing, "It is the very same Jesus," etc., and in breathless silence the congregation waited for further developments. I arose and announced for a text the words, "I speak as to wise men; judge ye what I say." I had a fairly free time in trying to place the consciousness of responsibility by showing that wisdom is the right use of knowledge, and that whether a person knows much or little he who fails to make a right use of the knowledge he has is not a wise man. I brought in the words of Jesus with reference to building on rock or on sand. At the close I gave opportunity for testimony. Sister Hart and Sister Coon spoke positively and definitely as to the power of God to save, and it was plainly evident that a change had come over the minds of the people. A pale, consumptive-looking woman, wearing about as much jewelry as could be made to hang on, arose at the back of the house and told how long she had been a professor of religion, how destitute of grace she was, and how anxiously she longed for a type of religion that would save her from her pride and sin. A noble-looking man arose and said, "This meeting puts me in mind of meetings I attended some years ago in Woodstock, Illinois, held by one Doctor Redfield;" and added, "Possibly there are some here to-night who knew him." I responded, "Yes, thank God!"

Our next chapter will show that the Master sometimes chooses a very unlikely donkey on which to ride into the fulfilment of the Father's will.

CHAPTER XII.

THE fine looking man and invalid woman mentioned
in our last chapter, who spoke in the meeting that
Saturday evening in the schoolhouse at Steamburg,
were John Ellison and his wife Eunice; and although
at that time they knew nothing of the Free Methodist church, they were in the providence of God to
become the chief agency in raising up the work in
that part of the state and to prove important factors
in the formation of the conference. Brother Ellison
was attending the Free-will Baptist college at Hillsdale and preaching to a church of that order a few
miles south of the city. On the Saturday of our
visit to Steamburg he, together with his wife, had
intended to get an early start and spend the day in
visiting among his members, but they were detained,
and being unable to get away from home until late
in the afternoon, they decided to stop with one of
his members at Steamburg until Sunday morning.
On his way from home someone informed Brother
Ellison that a woman was to speak at the schoolhouse that evening. Concluding that she must be
either a Spiritualist or an Adventist, he made up his

mind to attend the meeting and meet any erroneous teaching which might be advanced. He reached the schoolhouse just in time, as he passed through the gate, to hear the singing, "'Tis the very same Jesus." He said to himself, "There is no Adventism or Spiritualism about that." He went into the house and saw a man in the pulpit, and something about the spirit of the services brought to remembrance the meetings held by Doctor Redfield in Woodstock, Illinois, some years before. He afterwards told us that he attended the doctor's meetings because he liked to hear him preach, but somehow the truth did not get into his heart. But on that Saturday night in the schoolhouse his heart was opened and Doctor Redfield's preaching in its light and power flashed upon him.

At the close of the service Brother and Sister Ellison came to us and insisted upon our going to the place where they were stopping and spending the night there. Their host came up and seconded their request, but I told them I had three appointments for the next day and that I was dependent on this old gentleman for conveyance and could not go with them. Upon hearing that, Brother Ellison's friend said, "I have a good two-seated carriage and I will take you to your appointments." The way opening so clearly for us, we decided to stop with

Brother and Sister Ellison. My old friend was quite
put out at this and declared he would not come for
us in the morning, but I told him we would get to
the appointment, and he went on to the neighborhood where I was to preach the next morning. We
spent most of the night in talking with Brother and
Sister Ellison. They seemed eager to get the light.
In the morning when Sister Ellison came to the
breakfast table we noticed that the jewelry had been
laid aside. Brother Ellison had to go to his morning appointment, but said he would be at our afternoon meeting. Our morning appointment was at
the Black schoolhouse, the neighborhood I visited
when we stopped off at Osseo with our sick child.
In the afternoon I preached at what was called the
Blunt schoolhouse. Brother Ellison and wife and
several of their members were present.

I invited Brother Ellison to attend a grove-meeting we were to hold in about two weeks in the Jones
neighborhood near Ida station. He said if he could
possibly get away he would be with us at that meeting. I did not go to the evening appointment. It
was quite a distance, and being up so late the night
before we staid with a friend near the station, and in
the morning took the train at Osseo and returned to
Monroe county. The old gentleman and his daughter went on to the evening appointment, and I was

afterwards informed he told the people, "We are happily disappointed that Brother Hart is not here, and my daughter will now preach." This old man, who was the means of getting us into that section, was not long after arrested for crime and sentenced to several years imprisonment at Jackson. So the means used were unlikely, but the result was grand. Brother Ellison was with us at the grove-meeting near Ida. He earnestly sought the experience of a clean heart. His consecration was deep and thorough. On Monday morning just before he left for home he said, "Brother Hart, the Lord shows me that one of three things must take place—either my people must come up to this standard of salvation, or I must back down, or I must leave the Free-will Baptist church." I said to him, "Brother Ellison, all I ask of you, and I believe all that God asks of you, is not to back down." He answered firmly, "By the grace of God I will not." It was at this meeting that Sister Frink broke down and got blessed.

The grove-meeting over, Sister Hart and myself went on to attend the session of the Illinois conference held at Saint Charles, Illinois, Thursday, September 22, 1864. Joseph Jones was sent as lay delegate to represent the Michigan work. Henry Jones, although not present, was received into the traveling connection on trial. N. D. Fanning, C. S. Gitchell and M. V. Clute had been received on trial the year before and were continued. J. Miller and George H. Fox were admitted into full connection. This was the Brother Fox whose camp-meeting Brother Travis and I attended in Wisconsin in June, 1860. W. D. Bishop and J. E. Whiting were also received on trial at this session. At the beginning of this conference year Rev. J. W. Redfield, also Rev. Ira G. Gould, had passed away. At the request of the committee on memoirs Brother Roberts preached a sermon in memory of these devoted men of God. Brother Gould had come to us from the Wesleyan Methodist connection. He was a young man of uncommon promise. He commenced preaching at the age of eighteen. He was ordained by the Wesleyan church, but experienced the blessing of entire sanctification among our people. Someone tried to convince him that he had taken a wrong step in leaving the Wesleyan church and joining the Free Methodists and presented several strong reasons. Brother Gould listened attentively and then said, "I never took that view of the matter. With me it was a question of heaven or hell." He would get wonderfully blessed and jump, with his watch flying from his pocket and dangling by the cord. A denunciatory spirit was beginning to creep in, and I spent every moment I could spare from my work as secretary, with Brother Roberts, trying to devise some means by which it might be kept out. With the assistance of Brother Roberts I drew up the report on the state of the work, and after submitting it to Brother Travis and making the additions suggested by him presented it to the conference. This was the report:

Your committee beg leave to report as follows: We deem it of the first importance that we be united among ourselves. Having taken, by the grace of God, an uncomprising stand against all sin, having come out from the world, and therefore looking, according to the saying of Jesus, that the world will hate us—and having not only the pro-slavery and secret society influence, but the influence of the fashionable, formal churches of the day all combined against us, we feel deeply the necessity of union among ourselves. If we are united what can stand against us? But as our excellent Discipline says, in the 16th section of Chap. 3d, a section that we would do well to read and ponder, "If we divide we shall destroy ourselves, the work of God and the souls of our people." We must keep together; the necessity is imperative. That we may, let us see wherein we are united, and

1. We are Free Methodists. We hold to the common doctrines of Methodism. In particular we believe cordially in the doctrine of entire sanctification, and that it is an instantaneous work, attainable by faith.

2. The great end of our faith is the salvation of the soul. No earthly interest can bear any comparison to this; therefore our labors in private and public should be directly calculated to save souls and build them up in faith and holiness, We should make no conditions of salvation that are not found in the Word of God.

3. We believe that God does still answer prayer for the healing of the body, according to James v: 15, "And the prayer of faith shall save the sick." Methodist biographies contain too many well-authenticated cases, and too many instances have

occurred among us, for us to call this truth in question. But we do not believe that anyone has the power to heal whoever he pleases, or when he pleases. Nor is the gift of healing to be sought after as a distinct, specific blessing. This with all other spiritual gifts God divides to every man severally as he, God, will.

4. While we hold to being led by the Spirit, we do not believe that anyone is so fully led by it that he is not liable to make mistakes. Though the Spirit of God cannot err, we can, and we may think we are led by the Spirit when we are not. God's Spirit never leads us contrary to his Word, nor in a way to supercede the necessity of diligently searching the same that we may know the mind of the Lord.

5. We believe that modern spiritism is of the devil, and we have no sympathy with it in any of its forms and phases. Neither have we any fellowship with the heresies of Mormonism or the so-called latter-day saints.

6. Thus far we are agreed, and while we differ somewhat it may be in our modes of working, and in our judgment of the best method of dealing with such extravagances as have always manifested themselves in connection with a powerful work of God, still we will cherish the most cordial love and sympathy for each other, we will be more careful in believing reports to the prejudice of a brother, and when we hear them we will not relate them to others nor lay them up against him until we have communicated them to the brother to whom they refer and have received his explanation.

7. We would call attention to the indulgence of a spirit of ostentatious display, accompanied by a spirit of unhallowed bitterness which manifests itself in indiscriminate attacks upon the ministers and upon each other, breaking in upon the tried and established forms of worship, the bearing of blind burdens (see Wesley's sermon on evil speaking), at the same time neglecting to give private reproof according to Scripture rule, Matt. xviii. 15-17. Your committee believe were these things done away which render it impossible to keep the unity of the Spirit in the bonds of peace, we might consistently pray and

believe for those baptisms of the Spirit so necessary to carry on the work of God among us. Praying the great Head of the Church to give us mutual forbearance and a patient and teachable spirit, gentleness and meekness with all the fruits of the Spirit, we most respectfully submit the above.

The report was adopted, and for a time had the desired effect. Underwood, Dake and Ribble were ordained elders at this session. I think I have failed to state that I was ordained elder at the session held at Aurora the previous year. From my work in Michigan I reported one in full connection and thirty-eight on probation. The appointments for that year read, Michigan district, E. P. Hart, chairman and evangelist; Raisinville, W. D. Bishop, H. Jones.

We returned to Ida and with Brother W. D Bishop and wife went to housekeeping in rooms in the house of Jonathan Atkinson. Brother Bishop and Henry Jones filled the regular appointments, and my wife and myself went to regions beyond. One day while on our way to the old Baptist church spoken of before it seemed as though the powers of darkness had combined to hinder us, until finally I was constrained to cry out, "Lord Jesus, drive back the powers of hell." We made our way to the church, where a large congregation had assembled. The Lord came in wonderful power and there was a general break for the altar. We had intended to preach there only one evening, but it became so evident that this was the set time for God to favor Zion that I sent on and cancelled all other engagements and for four weeks held on at that point. This was a remarkable meeting in many respects. Some saw sights and some dreamed dreams, and the country was stirred for miles in every direction. One wicked man declared that as he passed the graveyard on his way from meeting he saw a ball of fire which shone so brightly that his horse was so frightened he could hardly urge him along. Women declared that their stoves shook, and the community was in a fever of excitement.

The ringleader in sin in the community near the close of the services one evening came marching down the aisle to the pulpit where I was standing inviting seekers forward, and in an excited tone said, "I want to ask you a question." I said, "Very well;" and he cried out, "I know there is the right and the wrong. I know there is a heaven and a hell. I want to shun one and gain the other, but I am without feeling. What am I to do?" I replied: "My dear sir, that very desire is begotten by the Spirit of God. Cherish it and you can be saved." Turning toward his comrades in the back of the house, with a wave of his hand he cried out, "Farewell," and fell on his knees at the penitent form. This was in the neighborhood where Mr. and Mrs. Frink lived. We were kindly entertained at their house during the meeting. Mrs. Frink kept getting out into the light and prayed earnestly for her husband. While he did not move out very rapidly it required no great degree of spiritual discernment to see that the woe was on him and that he must sooner or later yield to the claims of God. Not many months passed before, with their horse and buggy, little girl and gripsacks, they were out proclaiming the great salvation. At the close of the meeting, instead of at once forming a class, I told them that no preventing providence I would be around in about three weeks and that any who after considering the matter might desire to unite with us could at that time have the opportunity. Ordinarily this might be leaving open too much of a gap, but in this instance it made the converts all the more anxious to join.

During this time a preacher of another denomination came along and preached and informed the people that their latch-string always hung out. But the converts waited for our return and I informed them that we did not hang out our latch-string long enough for the world and the devil to come in and wanted only live fish, such as could swim against the current. I do not remember the number taken in, but a good society was formed. This for years has been a permanent appointment and our people used the old Baptist church until they built a house of their own. A son and daughter of Sister Lewis were saved in this meeting, also a Mrs. Irish whose husband was away in the army. On his return, in a meeting held here by B. R. Jones, he was grandly saved and for years was one of our sweetest spirited and most efficient preachers.

Years afterwards the Methodists made flattering proposals to a son of Brother Irish who desired to fit himself for the ministry, and the going of the son drew the father also; I regret to be obliged to add that Brother Irish yielding to the influences by which he was surrounded joined the Masons and became dead and formal.

CHAPTER XIII.

IN COMPANY with Henry Jones we went up on the Huron river and opened up the work in that region. One evening at the close of the service in a school-house a man came up to me and in an excited tone inquired, "What is your name, and where are you from, and where are you going?" I answered, "My name is E. P. Hart, I am from Illinois, and I am going to heaven." He further inquired, "How do you live?" I replied' "Spiritually, on the bread of heaven; physically, on meat, bread and potatoes." That man was not long in getting into the fountain, and ever after Job Burnap was careful to see that provision for our physical man was not wanting.

My wife and I were driving one day on a corduroy road through a swamp, when the horse became nervous and well-nigh unmanageable. Getting out of the buggy, I took the animal by the bit, patted her, spoke encouragingly to her, and succeeded in leading her quietly across. As we afterwards learned from the men themselves, two brothers by the name of French were out in the swamp that afternoon hunting, and unknown to us were looking on as I persuaded the animal quietly across the rough place. They at once said, "That must be the new preacher and his wife, who are holding meetings at the school-house. We'll go up to-night and hear him." They went, were brought under the convincing power of the truth and Spirit, and were soundly converted. They joined the church and remained reliable members to the day of death. They afterwards said to Sister Hart, "If your husband had spoken harshly or struck that horse we never would have gone near your meeting."

Uncle Horace Ash was a man of God and known all through that section. In some way years before he had received the light and had been brought out into the experience of entire sanctification. When we went into his neighborhood he at once recognized the joyful sound and immediately fell into line. His brother, known as Uncle Arby wanted to be good but lacked the experience. He diligently sought the Lord and with his large family of sons helped materially in establishing the work in that part of the State. His son Jim never seemed to have the confidence to claim saving grace but he was none the less ready to help on the work. A number of times when we were without conveyance and wanted to get from one neighborhood to another Jim would come up at the close of the service and

say slyly, "Brother Hart, my team is on the altar."
Several appointments were established and Brother
Bishop and wife moved to that post and took charge
of the work.

In the spring we held a grove-meeting in one of
the neighborhoods. Living near by was a man known
as Uncle Johnny Clark. He held the office of
justice of the peace. He was a kind-hearted man
but addicted to the liquor habit, a fearful slave to
tobacco, and years before in the amputation of one
of his legs had contracted the opium habit. Further
he was a staunch Democrat, one of the old school,
who could hardly believe that a "nigger" had a soul.
We closed the grove-meeting with the afternoon
service. Conviction was on the people all through
the community. Brother Bishop gave out an
appointment for the evening at the schoolhouse.
Although Uncle Johnny Clark did not attend the
grove-meeting on his crutch and his wooden leg he
hobbled over to the evening meeting at the schoolhouse and earnestly sought salvation. The Lord
heard the poor man cry and delivered him from his
trouble. He went on in experience until cleansed
from all filthiness of flesh and spirit. The last time
I heard Uncle Johnny testify was at a quarterly
meeting we held in the Wesleyan Methodist church
on the "old plank road." With streaming eyes,

leaning on his crutch, the old gentleman told how God had saved him from tobacco, whiskey and opium, and then added, "As I was driving to town the other day I saw a colored man coming, and something said to me, 'That man is your brother,' and as he came up I bowed to him and he bowed very respectfully, and oh how God blessed me!" Uncle Johnny died not long after and went to join the innumerable company "who have gotten the victory over the beast and over his image and over his mark and over the number of his name, and who stand on the sea of glass, having the harps of God."

From the grove-meeting near Ida, Rev. John Ellison returned to Hillsdale and began to preach holiness to his people. For a few Sabbaths there was no visible opposition, and several of his members began to seek the experience. But before many weeks had passed a society meeting was held and Brother Ellison was notified that they did not care to have his services as pastor any longer. Upon this, several of the members who had gotten out into the light withdrew from the society and Brother Ellison preached to them at the Blunt schoolhouse. After awhile they began to feel that they ought to have a home. Most of them were in favor of joining the Free Methodist church, and Brother Ellison's sympathies were in that direction, but he thought the time had not

yet come for him to take the step. He finally wrote
me informing me how matters stood, and stated that
while he did not feel like joining us at present he
thought if I would make them a visit several would
unite and if I organized a class and so desired he
would preach for them. I at once went, and on
Sabbath morning preached at the Blunt schoolhouse.
I then read and explained our Discipline. Brother
Ellison seemed quite uneasy, and as I was about to
give opportunity for any who might desire to join to
step out and answer the questions, Brother Ellison
stepped up and whispered in my ear, "Go ahead,
Brother Hart, I'll go the whole hog." Not a very
elegant, but quite an expressive way of signifying his
determination to join. So we formed quite a class,
and Brother Ellison was duly installed as pastor.
From this beginning our work spread through the
western part of the state. Ira W. Bell, for years one
of our most efficient and most reliable preachers, also
Brothers Mabbs, Leisenring and others, were raised
up. Some have remained with us, some have felt
called to go elsewhere and some have been called to
their eternal reward. A Sister M. was prominent
among those of Brother Ellison's members who got
saved and came with our people. Her husband was
in the army. He was a member of the Free-will
Baptist church. When he returned home and learned

of the step his wife had taken he was greatly dis-
pleased and was full of fault-finding. These things
came to my ears, and seeing him in the congregation
one day I took occasion in some advice I was giving
to say: "There are some people who, if they would
spend half as much time in prayer as they do in
fault-finding, would get along better in their experience." The shot went to the intended mark. At
the close of the service the man came up, and putting
a dollar in my hand thanked me for the advice and
said he would try to profit by it. He got saved
and lived and died a member of one of our conferences.

The way opened and our work spread out into
Branch county. South Quincy became a rallying
point. Sylvester Forbes, from Illinois, the eccentric
preacher spoken of before, came over to Michigan
and held meetings at different points. He was a
peculiar looking man, very effeminate in appearance,
having a voice like a woman's and was a good singer.
He held a meeting in the schoolhouse at South
Quincy. Living in the neighborhood was a family
by the name of Nichols. The wife was a strong
Baptist. John, the husband, made no profession.
John was busy in his sap-bush and would not attend
meeting, but the eccentricities of the preacher were
so much talked about that John, one Sunday evening

after working all day carrying sap, concluded he
would go and hear the man. The preacher went on
to tell how cheaply some people would sell their
souls. "Why," he exclaimed, "there is a man in this
community who will sell his soul for a pail of sap!"
Something said to John, "Thou art the man," and he
began earnestly to seek salvation.

Sister Nichols was a great stickler for immersion,
and was a good deal troubled because the Free
Methodist church was not exclusive on that line.
But the Lord cleared the matter all up for her. She
had a beautiful boy baby, and concluded to dedicate
him to God in infant baptism. "Now," said she, "I
am a Free Methodist. I was immersed in water, in
the baptism of the Holy Ghost the Spirit was poured
on me, and my baby is sprinkled. I have all the
three modes."

In that community we had several of the most
powerful camp-meetings I ever attended. Our camp-
meetings of those days were of the primitive order.
Each family had its own tent, made of common
"factory" and interlined with sheets. The frame was
of poles cut in the grove. We had no tabernacle,
but had a rough stand for a pulpit, so constructed
that twenty or more preachers could sleep in the
back part, and this also answered for a temporary
jail in which any roughs who persisted in disturb-

ing the services might be confined until the proper
official could come and take them away for trial.
But in the large number of camp-meetings we held,
I do not recall more than two or three instances in
which we were obliged to resort to force to keep
order. We usually had so much going on at the
altar that the attention of all classes was held to so
late an hour that they were glad to go home for rest.
We had large "fire stands," one at each corner of the
ground inside the circle of tents. These were built
with four upright posts, supporting a platform about
four feet square. The platform was covered with
earth, and on this a bright fire of dry wood was kept
burning at night during the services. / Lighted in
this way, with the blaze from the fire stands streaming up among the branches of the tall beech and
maple trees, a congregation of perhaps one or two
thousand seated on planks laid across log stringers,
the preacher in the stand at one time in thunder
tones declaring the mandates of Sinai and then in
accents of sweetest mercy pleading with sinners to
turn to God, the saints with glory beaming from
their countenances and the heavenly light flashing
from their eyes, ever and anon encouraging the
speaker with their glad responses of "Hallelujah"
and "Glory to God"—all together, in spirit at least,
went to make up a scene akin to the Revelator's

description of the happy, blood-washed throng around the throne.

Our services in those days were on the "old line" of meekness and brotherly love, each esteeming others better than himself. There was an entire absence of that denunciatory, criticising spirit which in later years crept in and in some parts made our work a hissing and a reproach—a spirit which led people to turn their eyes from the pit of the hole from which they had been digged, and, blinding them to ther own frailties and weaknesses, turned their argus gaze on the infirmities and failures of others. In Romans 12: 16 the apostle says, "Be not wise in your own conceits." It certainly is bad enough for a person to be filled with conceit, but when a person becomes "wise in his own conceits" this is deplorable indeed. I remember but one instance in which in those days this spirit manifested itself, and that was in the case of a preacher who came to us from another denomination. He attended one of our Quincy camp-meetings and felt called to straighten us out. He went on until he got to red-topped boots and hat bands, and I felt it was time to call a halt. Going up into the stand, I called the attention of the people to the possibility of tithing the mint and cummin and anise to the neglect of the weightier matters of the law. I said, "Take for in-

stance the matter of coat collars, for I see you all
have collars to your coats. But," I said, "some of
you may say, 'Brother Hart, that is too small a matter.' Is it?" I inquired, "let us see." Then I went
on to make an estimate of one-quarter of a yard of
cloth in each collar—so many millions of coats—the
number of yards of cloth at so much a yard and the
amount at a moderate estimate was immense. "And
now," I said, "so much for coat collars, to say nothing of coat tails." The preacher was highly indignant and "went away in a rage." But the next year
he came back and told us that before he got beyond
the sound of the meeting something said to him,
"You are a fool." He made his humble confession
and struck the "old line" of meekness and love.
Whatever else I may be responsible for, I disclaim
all responsibility for this egotistical spirit.

CHAPTER XIV.

A PAPER has come to my hand bringing to mind incidents which might have been presented sooner, but which under the license of digression may be brought in here.

In June, 1862, my wife and myself, at the earnest request of Brother Roberts, went east from Illinois and attended the Bergen camp-meeting, the last meeting held by our people on the old Bergen camp-ground. There was a good number of tents and a large attendance. Here for the first time and only time I saw Loren Stiles and Fay Purdy. Brother Stiles, as I remember him, was a tall, spare man with an intellectual cast of countenance and the look of an orator. He was in poor health and I did not have the privilege of hearing him preach. It was evident that Purdy had lost his grip. He seemed himself to realize this, to some extent at least, for one morning in the love-feast he said, "I feel I need a new touch. my sword is getting rusty." He seemed quite anxious to get an expression of Sister Hart's opinion of himself, and finally she said, "To speak plainly, I am a good deal disappointed in you,

Brother Purdy. I had heard so much about your power and discernment of spirit, I don't know about the sword getting rusty. I think before the Lord will allow it to become rusty he will take it away." He took it well, but seemed considerably troubled.

I think Father Abell had the general oversight of the meeting. The Nazarite element was pretty strongly represented and there was a spirit of restraint for fear of an outbreak of fanaticism. Blind Henry was present. A brother one day came up and speaking to him, said, "This is Brother Henry, the blind preacher, is it?" "No," was the answer, "I am a blind man, but thank God I am not a blind preacher." Here for the first time, but not the last, I saw Joseph McCreery. He was a peculiar looking man, his heavy eyebrows overshadowing small, twinkling, black eyes which seemingly were ever on the lookout for the ludicrous. The oratory of Stiles or the inexorable logic of Roberts were not more feared and dreaded by the Regency than was the cutting sarcasm of Joseph McCreery.

It was a damp, dismal evening at the close of a cold, rainy day, when some one came to me and said no one was willing to preach and asked if I would try it. I said I would do the best I could. There were no fires on the fire stands and aside from that which was to emanate from the speaker we depended for light on two or three tallow candles in the preachers' stand. As usual when the circumstances are most unfavorable and we have the least of the help of the Spirit the louder we "holler," so for thirty minutes or more I strained my voice in trying to preach. At the close of my effort I went to the Buffalo tent where I was stopping. Brother Roberts stood at the entrance of the tent talking with a man, and, as I approached, said, "Brother Hart, this is Brother Joseph McCreery." "Why," I said, "Brother McCreery, for a long time I have wanted to see you. How do you do?" Raising his shaggy eyebrows, he looked at me and said, "Was that you 'hollering' so out there?" I replied, "Yes, sir. I was trying to preach." "Well," he said, "I stood it as long as I could and came away." Laughingly I answered, "Well, I honor your judgment."

Joseph and Benjamin, these two brethren usually called each other—these were their given names. Brother Roberts inquired, "Joseph, why didn't you come to camp-meeting sooner?" "Had to shear my sheep," was the reply. "Sheep?" said Brother Roberts, "How many sheep have you?" With all seriousness he answered, "One." Going into the tent and taking seats Brother Roberts inquired, "What are you doing these days, Joseph?" Brother

McCreery replied, " I am living at home and we have religion twice a day at our house." "And what are you doing, Benjamin?" inquired McCreery. With a good deal of earnestness Brother Roberts replied, " I am going through this land for God and salvation the best I can." "That's right," quickly replied McCreery, "I tell you this old pool of Methodism better be stirred by a bullfrog jumping into it than to remain stagnant." But more of this eccentric man anon.

James Vick, the noted seedsman, and his devoted wife, were at the meeting, and strongly urged Sister Hart to go with them to their home in Rochester, while with Brother Roberts and Travis I went on to another camp-meeting. Sister Hart, however, decided to go and visit an aunt living at Attica. We went on to a meeting held at Union, New York. Here we had to encounter a tent of fanatics calling themselves Nazarites. They kept pretty closely to their tent, shouting and having the most distressing manifestations, only coming out occasionally to berate and ridicule those of us who were laboring in the meeting. Here Brother Roberts held a session of the Susquehanna conference.

From this meeting I returned to Buffalo, where my wife met me. We spent a day in Buffalo, and among other places visited a large Catholic cathedral.

We gazed on the paintings of the saints, but what affected us most was a life-size image of Christ in wax. It represented him as lying in the tomb. The image was so real in appearance that our emotions were greatly stirred, when speaking to my wife I said, "Martha, our's is a living Christ." Some time after at a camp-meeting at which Joseph Terrill was present, by way of illustration I related the incident which, it seems, made such an impression on Brother Terrill's mind and heart that he penned the following lines and sent them to us. They have for a long time been mislaid, but, as I stated at the beginning of this chapter, having providentially come to my hand these recollections are the result.

A LIVING CHRIST.

BY JOSEPH GOODWIN TERRILL.

Two travelers, a man and wife,
Were wandering through cathedral vast,
Of lofty dome and transept great,
With eyes intently fixed on saints,
The creatures of a painter's skill.
They came at last to molded form
Of Christ in wax. It lay in state,
Life size, beneath a vase of glass;
The face, the limbs, attested full
The artist's power. And as they gazed
The wax seemed flesh, just parted from
The soul. The print of nails in palm
And foot, and print of cruel spear,
And wound of thorn upon the brow,

Seemed fresh as done but yesterday.
The features fair bore trace of pain,
And agony extreme, but mixed
With pity, as for those for whom
All this was borne.   The posture of
The prostrate form, the silence of
The place, were calculated all
T' impress the mind with solemn awe
And heartfelt sympathy.   But few
Could gaze with critic's eye upon
That scene, and not lose sight of friends,
Of passers-by, and all of earth,
In contemplation of the pious thought
Designed.   No wonder then, that when
These Christians gazed upon the scene,
The woman's heart was touched, and tears
Came gushing from her eyes.   Her Christ
Seemed there, just crucified, for sins
Not of his own, but of the world's.
The husband saw the heaving breast,
The trickling tear, and whisp'ring said,
"Our's, Martha, is a living Christ."
"Oh, Edward, yes; thank God!" she cried,
And dashed the tears away.

At the end of the long bridge, just across the
Raisin river from Brother Atkinson's was a church
building known as the "White church."   It belonged
originally, I believe, to the Congregationalists, but
for some years there had been no organization there
and no regular services.   In January, 1865, I think it
was, Brother Bishop and myself held a series of
revival services in this church.   Sister Hart had a
short time previously gone home to her father's in

Illinois. Brother and Sister Bishop and myself, together with members of our church living along the river, were the laborers in the meeting. We had large congregations and deep conviction was settling down upon the people.

Near the church lived one John N. He had formerly been a class-leader in the Methodist Episcopal church, but for some years had been a rabid Spiritualist. He would persist in speaking in the meetings, claiming to be moved by the spirit of a dead Indian. As this was bringing in distraction, as he arose one evening to speak I stopped him when, with an air of injured innocence, he inquired, "Can't I be allowed to speak in the meeting?" I replied, "If you want to come forward and confess your sins and get saved you can do so, but we will have none of your dead Indian talk here, for," I added, "Spiritualism is all of the devil." He at once spoke up and said, "Will you give us a sermon on the subject, sir?" Without taking a second thought, I at once replied, "Yes, sir, by the grace of God the subject for to-morrow night will be, 'Spiritualism gone to seed.'" At the close of the service, as we passed out of the church, the man said to me, "Give us a good one, Mr. Hart." I answered, "I will do the best I can, Mr. N." Having thus publicly committed myself, the consciousness of responsibility drove me to my Bible and to my knees. I slept but little that night and spent the following day in fasting, prayer and diligent searching of the word.

That night the church was packed. For a text I announced the following words: "And when they shall say unto you, Seek unto them that have familiar spirits and unto wizards that peep and that mutter: should not a people seek unto their God? for the living to the dead? To the law and to the testimony: if they speak not according to this word, it is because there is no light in them." Isa. 8: 19, 20. I spoke first of the difficulty in combating error, as it consists largely in a denial of truth, and as it is not committed to any definite and positive line it is much like a fox in a field, when cornered in one it jumps the fence into another. I then divided Spiritualists into two classes, those who do and those who do not profess belief in the Bible. Both classes were in that part of the state, for in a gathering not long before this the anti-Bible class had denounced the word of God and thrown it down on the floor and publicly stamped upon it. But this man N. claimed to believe in the Bible, and that it taught Spiritualism. So I said, "With those who denounce the Bible I have no controversy to-night but shall deal entirely with those who claim to believe in it." "To the law and to the testimony, if they speak not according to this word it

is because there is no light in them." I had made a
note of every passage from beginning to end in the
Bible which spoke of wizards, necromancers, witches,
evil spirits and demons. I read and commented on
these passages, showing that God invariably pronounced a curse upon them.

For once at least I was master of the situation.
God endorsed the truth, the Spirit broke on the congregation and a crowd rushed to the altar, among
the number a daughter of Mr. N., who came
literally screaming down the aisle. Sister Hart, a
short time before, at her father's in Illinois, dreamed
of our meeting and thought she saw a huge serpent
writhing around among us, and that finally Brother
Bishop and myself got it cornered and killed it.
Whether there was anything in the dream or not, it
is certain that the slimy snake of Spiritism was throt-
tled in that community. The meeting went on in
power and a fine class was organized at the White
church. A few weeks after the close of the meeting I
went on to Illinois, and during the month of March
assisted in revival services at Aurora. On the evening of the 22nd, just as I was about to start for meeting, a telegram from Marengo was handed me, and
on opening it I read this brief but significant dis-
patch, "Girl—all doing well." So a bright, black-
eyed daughter was added to our family circle.

Not long after, I returned to Michigan and labored until the Saint Charles camp-meeting, in June, which my wife and I attended, and soon after with our babies went back to Michigan. We arranged to start for Michigan on a certain train, but there came up a terrific thunder-storm, and, thoroughly drenched, we reached the depot just in time to see the train move off. We returned to Father Bishop's and waited for the night train, which we succeeded in reaching. We passed through Chicago, when I discovered I was short of funds, but as the train stopped at a station in Michigan a lady of our acquaintance came aboard, and spying us came up and put a five dollar bill in my hand. So we understood the providence by which we missed the train, and thanked God and took courage.

We labored through the remainder of the summer and went back to the session of the Illinois conference held at Marengo, September 13-18, 1865. I was again elected secretary, with T. S. La Due as assistant. As lay delegates from the Michigan conference this year we had L. T. Frink and John Ellison to represent the work. These brethren were received into the conference on trial, and H. L. Jones and W. D. Bishop were continued. We reported from Michigan about two hundred in full connection and on probation. The appointments for this year read:

"Michigan and Indiana district, E. P. Hart, chairman; Huron, H. L Jones; Raisinville, Lemuel Frink;
Morenci, to be supplied; Van Buren. to be supplied;
Ransom, W. D. Bishop; Coldwater, John Ellison."
So I had six appointments on my district. I held
the quarterly meetings on these and labored in raising up new circuits. During the winter our work
extended over into Ohio and Indiana.

In the fall of 1865 we received a call from two
brethren living near Morenci, Lenawee county,
Michigan, to come and hold meetings. We sent for
our household goods which to this time had been
left in Illinois. We had them shipped to Clayton,
the nearest railroad station, and went on to settle
down in that part of the state for the winter and try
to open up the work. We found that Brothers
Osgood and Goss had secured a large farm house
two or three miles west of Morenci in which we were
to live. We moved in our goods and found ourselves very comfortably situated, only that we had
no very near neighbors, the nearest one being a
partially insane man, bearing the reputation of a bad
and dangerous character. As I had to be away
from home a good deal on the district this made it
unpleasant for Sister Hart with her two small children. Anticipating this we had secured Florence
Plues, one of the twin girls saved in our meeting

in the Plues schoolhouse, to go and live with us as companion for Sister Hart. But Florence never before having been away from home was severely attacked with that unpleasant and distressing disease called home-sickness and we were obliged to allow her to return home, so Sister Hart had to take on courage and, trusting in the Lord, stay alone with the children during my absence.

Brothers Osgood and Goss were strongly opposed to Masonry and there was a strong anti-Masonic sentiment in the community generally. But with exceptions of these two brethren and a Brother Reid living in another neighborhood there was little pretension to piety. When we were fairly settled a "bee" was announced and men from that and adjoining neighborhoods came together and with a horse-power saw prepared beech and maple stove-wood sufficient for the winter. But this zeal, being begotten by a partisan spirit while quite acceptable and helpful for a supply of fuel for the winter, did not contribute especially to the spiritual interests of the work. During the time I could spare from my district work I went out through the country looking up appointments. Grandpa Goss, as he was familiarly known, had a white horse and light democrat wagon which were placed at my disposal, and with this rig I went out looking for "openings." A few

miles from our home I found a vacant Presbyterian
church and looking up one of the elders arranged
for stated appointments. At our first appointment
we found the choir in the gallery ready with the organ
to bear some humble part in the exercises. I announced my hymns and they lead off seemingly
under the supposition that they were conferring a
great favor upon the new preacher. I allowed it
to pass for that time, but at our next service I gave
out my opening hymn and saying, "Let all join
in the singing," I lead off myself. The people
seemed well pleased to have congregational singing, but the choir were very indignant and ever
after took their seats in the body of the church
and stoutly refused to take any part. I preached
at this church for some time, but finding more
promising openings finally canceled my appointments. Something of an interest being awakened
the "elder" concluding it would be a good time
to revive their services, went around to see what
the people would contribute to the support of a
regular pastor, and nearly all assured him they would
assist provided we would secure the man who had
been preaching there of late. The elder came to me
and proposed to engage me as regular pastor, but I
informed the good brother that my time was so fully
occupied I could not take the position. I got an

appointment in a schoolhouse about three miles east of Morenci, where a people calling themselves Christians had a society and a regular service. I called the place a Campbellite swamp. I preached there a few times when the Campbellite preacher came around and in preaching said, "The Holy Ghost, what kind of a ghost is that?" "It is," said he "a spooky, scary thing." These people at first treated our meetings with the utmost contempt. Someone of them sent me a note requesting me to preach from one of two texts. One of the texts called for a verse from a chapter in John not having as many verses as the number of the one called for. The other text read as follows, "Then Peter said unto them, Repent, and be baptized every one of you in the name of Jesus Christ for the remission of sins and ye shall receive the gift of the Holy Ghost" (Acts 2: 38). At the appointment the next evening I read the note requesting me to preach from one of two texts, and then said, "As there are not as many verses in the chapter of John as the note calls for, it is Hobson's choice with me, and I must use the other text or none." I said, "In considering this text in Acts 2: 38 there are three things mentioned, namely, 'Repentance,' 'Baptism' and the 'gift of the Holy Ghost.'" "Now," I said, "If any one of these is of less importance than the other that one is baptism, but there is a certain class of so-called disciples who jump over repentance into some goose pond in so-called baptism and wholly ignore the gift of the Holy Ghost, but to-night," I said, "we will start in with repentance and if time permits consider the other parts of the text also." They were greatly stirred and some went out in a rage. As they passed out I said, "That's right, as fast as you are dressed up you can pass out, for by the grace of God I pre-pose to cut garments for you all to-night." The Lord endorsed the truth and many were brought under conviction. The Lord came in saving power and these people were at least whipped into respect for after the services nights we could hear them saying among themselves, "Well, I didn't ridicule the Holy Ghost."

We finally appointed a watch-night service for New Year's eve. Brother W. D. Bishop and wife came from the Ransom circuit, where he was preaching, to assist in the meeting. Brother Bishop and myself had gone on to the neighborhood where the watch service was to be held, and Grandpa Goss with "Jim", the old white horse, and the democrat wagon went to our house to bring Sister Bishop, my wife and our two children. Sister Hart with the baby in her arms sat with Grandpa Goss on the spring seat in front, while Sister Bishop with the

other child seated on a board across the wagon-box
realized the benefit of the spring of the rear axletree.
By dark the people came streaming in from all
directions, and long before the hour for the service
to begin the house was crowded. Sister Hart made
a bed for the children on the desks, and we commenced our meeting. Aside from two or three who
might pray or speak, Brother and Sister Bishop and
my wife and myself were the only ones to carry on
the meeting, but the good Lord came by his Spirit,
and with a sermon by Brother Bishop and two by
myself and prayers and testimonies of our wives and
others the time was fully occupied, and instead of
silent prayer at the midnight hour we had a penitent
form filled with earnest seekers.

Early in the spring, as I was so far from the
main part of our work and as the brethren were
anxious to have us more centrally located, we concluded we had better remove to Monroe county.
Sending word to the brethren that we were ready to
come, Brother Jonathan Atkinson, a son of Brother
Plues, and a son of Brother Jones, each with a team
came to take our goods to Raisinville. The night
they reached our house there came a heavy fall of
snow, and it looked as though they were storm-
bound, but by the exercise of a little inventive
genius they soon improvised pole-sleds, and piling

wagons and goods on to these made a successful trip of nearly fifty miles through the drifts. Grandpa Goss took me and wife and the two children to Clayton to take the train. Just as he left us at the station he slipped a five dollar bill into my hand. The train was several hours late, and when it did arrive the conductor gruffly informed us that we could not get through to Ida that night; but deciding to go as far as we could, we boarded the train and went on to Adrian, to find that our train for Ida had already gone. I now found use for the money Brother Goss had given me, and going to a hotel near the station succeeded in securing a warm room. So severe was the storm that no train left Adrian until 4 p. m. the following day. We finally reached our destination in safety and moved into a parsonage near the White church in Raisinville which the brethren had bought, the first Free Methodist parsonage in Michigan. While living here our larder became exceeding low and we hardly knew how we were to get along, but one day we received a letter, and on opening it a five dollar bill fell out, and from the letter we read, "From a friend to help roll the old chariot along." Funds kept coming in, so we were soon prepared to meet the extra expense of our coming camp-meeting.

CHAPTER XV.

IN JUNE, 1866, we held a camp-meeting in a grove near the Raisin river, just a short distance above Brother Atkinson's. This was a remarkable meeting. It proved to be the means of advertising our work pretty much through the entire state. Reporters came up from Monroe. The reporter for the Republican paper gave a most ridiculous account of the exercises. He said that the people cut the pigeon wing and danced Jim Crow, and that the meeting was a perfect pandemonium. The Democrat paper took it up and said if it was a pandemonium it was such a pandemonium as they had on the day of Pentecost, and further expressed surprise that a Republican paper should come out against these people, for if the Free Methodist preachers in the state of Michigan should leave the Republican party that party would be in a hopeless minority. This statement was the more remarkable as at that time our preachers did not number more than a half dozen. But this all tended to awaken curiosity, and we received calls from all directions to come and labor.

The Michigan conference was organized June 22, 1866, in connection with the camp-meeting held on the Raisin river. The conference was organized in a brick schoolhouse near the camp-ground. Brother Roberts was present and presided. I was elected secretary. The following preachers were received into full connection from the Illinois conference: H. L. Jones, C. S. Gitchell, W. D. Bishop and E. P. Hart. John Ellison and L. T. Frink were received from the Illinois conference, with credit for one year on trial in that conference.

Six preachers were received on trial; of this number were three brothers by the name of Riley. They were men of some preaching ability and labored quite acceptably, especially William, who opened up the work at Moreville and other points. During the summer one of them got into difficulty with the United States custom house at Detroit, and was expelled. The others, out of sympathy with their brother, withdrew. Living a few miles from Moreville was an old English couple by the name of East. They had belonged with the Ranters in England. Their son attended William Riley's meeting, and went home and reported that the Ranters had come. The old people were not slow in getting to the services. They were so overjoyed they could not refrain from giving audible expression to their feelings.

of delight. These old people stood by the work till death called them to their reward. Their children were converted, a church was built at Moreville, also one in the East neighborhood, and several strong circuits raised up in that section. William, the eldest son, who first reported the meeting to his parents, remained a true man of God to his death, which took place recently in the northern part of the state.

We had a short conference year, but during the time the first Free Methodist church in Michigan was built, at Sherwood, Branch county, under the labors of Rev. John Ellison. Brother and Sister Frink had a successful term on the Huron circuit. One year, while Brother Bishop was preaching on the Huron work, in quite a remarkably providential manner he received needed financial help. They had bought a new stove, but were obliged to run in debt to the amount of six or seven dollars. They had managed to get a dollar or two ahead, and started to drive to Detroit and make a payment. Out in the field, as they were driving along, they saw a large, strange-looking bird. Brother Bishop siezed the blanket and halter, and running towards the bird saw that it was a huge eagle. As though held by a spell, the eagle stood perfectly still, and Brother Bishop, throwing the blanket over its head, soon had it captive. With the halter he bound it in the back of his buggy and went on to Detroit. Showing the bird there, a man who kept a meat-market became quite anxious to purchase it, and finally offered seven dollars, which offer was readily accepted, and Brother Bishop went in and paid the balance due on his stove. The bird had been caught so easily, the market man concluded it could not fly, so taking it out one day he let it stand unbound, when stretching out its great wings it soared toward the sun—but the purpose had been fulfilled, the preacher's necessities had been met.

The work extended along what was known as the Ridge Road, in Monroe and Lenawee counties. In the East neighborhood was a family by the name of Gray. The old gentleman took a decided stand. He was a highly intellectual man and carried a strong influence for the right. Sister Eunice Gray, his son's wife, fell into line and, although her husband made no profession, their large farmhouse has ever been a pilgrim home. Of late they have spent the winters in Florida, and since this series of articles was commenced Sister Gray has written Sister Hart and myself of the hallowed recollections of those days of blessing of thirty-five years ago.

The second session of our conference was held in the new church, at Sherwood, Branch county, giving

a conference year of six months. Brother Joseph
Travis presided. He also preached the dedicatory
sermon. It was a remarkable one from the text,
"The glory of this latter house shall be greater than
the former, saith the Lord of hosts; and in this place
will I give peace, saith the Lord of hosts" (Hag. 2:
9). Our membership at this session numbered four
hundred and eighty-two. I was again elected chairman, and had a district of nine circuits. Brothers
Frink and Ellison were received into full connection. I was elected ministerial and John Plues lay
delegate to the second session of the general conference, which convened at Buffalo, New York, Wednesday, October 10, 1866. After the first Sabbath, the
conference adjourned to Albion. The Michigan
conference had but two delegates, but with the help
of Brother Plues we made noise and stir enough for
half a dozen. I remember one evening in Buffalo,
when Brother Plues got blessed, and hooted and
yelled in his characteristic way, the police came
rushing in, seemingly supposing that some one was
being murdered, but they soon took in the situation
and passed out leaving us alone in our glory.

Joseph McCreery had settled on a small farm in
Van Buren county, Michigan. He attended one of
our camp-meetings, held at Quincy, and there publicly acknowledged that he had made a mistake in

opposing the organization of the Free Methodist church, and, turning to Brother Roberts, who was present, said, "Brother Roberts, you were wiser than I." He sold out in Michigan, and in the fall of 1865, united with the Illinois conference and was appointed to Marengo. I remember that Brother Terrill presented the name of C. H. Lovejoy, of the Methodist Episcopal church in Kansas, for reception into the conference. Brother Lovejoy was not present, but Brother Terrill had his picture and passed that around among the members of the conference. Brother Lovejoy was received. The name of Joseph McCreery was then presented, and Brother Roberts inquired whether he wished to say anything to the conference, when he arose, and, raising his eyebrows, said, "Brethren, I haven't any picture, but you can look at me."

In 1866 Brother McCreery was one of the ministerial delegates from the Illinois conference to the general conference which met at Buffalo of which I have already spoken. I learned that he was advocating the election of two superintendents and suggesting my name for the second one. I hunted him up and protested against any such action and finally said, "Brother McCreery, I don't like such work in a general conference, it looks too much like log-rolling." His reply was, "I don't know who has a better right to roll the log than the man who cut down the tree." After some years Brother McCreery dropped our of the traveling connection and went out to Nebraska where he took up a claim and for a time, no doubt, was sadly down in his experience. He finally sold out and went to live with his youngest daughter in California. He got blessed in his soul and the residue of his days were spent in loving obedience to God.

The last characteristic speech I heard him make was at the last session of the California conference held by Brother Roberts. Towards the close of the session he arose and spoke in substance as follows: "When I was a little boy I lived on the farm with my grandfather. They had a hired girl by the name of Peggy. Grandfather and Uncle John would go over the hill to work, and when Peggy had dinner about ready she would take a great conch-shell and give a tremendous blast to call grandfather and Uncle John to dinner. They had a little yellow dog, and when Peggy would give a blast on the conch-shell the little yellow dog would whine and cry and lie down and roll over and take on fearfully. Finally someone told Peggy to put some soft soap in the conch-shell and then when she blew on it the yellow dog wouldn't take on so. The next time Peggy went to blow on the conch-shell she put in some soft soap and blew a great blubber. The yellow dog didn't whine or cry, but grandfather and Uncle John didn't come to dinner. "Now," said he, "boys, whatever you do don't put any soft soap in the gospel horn; let the yellow dogs howl, but have the trumpet give the certain sound." The old brother before the close of that conference session to a great extent lost his mind. In a few months he went east to live with his son at Elgin, Illinois, where he closed his eyes in peace and went to his eternal reward.

So these men who, by a heaven-quickened spiritual intuition, felt and saw the oncoming flood of worldliness, and by the help of God were enabled to raise up a standard against it, one by one are passing away, and it now devolves on us who are coming to the front, in love and meekness to maintain the principles of righteousness to which they consecrated their powers and in defense of which they stood while they lived.

CHAPTER XVI.

THE winter of 1866-67 we labored at Windsor, a small burg out about six miles from Mansfield, Richland county, Ohio. Our children were with their grandparents in Illinois. Our congregations were large, the people coming in from the country around. A number were saved. We made our home most of the time with a family by the name of Garrison. The old people were saved in the early part of the meeting. A man and wife by the name of Nyman living in the same neighborhood, who claimed to be strong Universalists, were brought under conviction. By invitation we went to their house, and nearly all the night could hear Mrs. Nyman sobbing and groaning on account of her sins. They were clearly converted and became strong members.

We had a young man by the name of Ash preaching on the work. He was a son of Uncle Arby Ash, who lived on the Huron work in Michigan. This young man in giving notice of our coming had given occasion for a great many humorous remarks, for he had repeatedly advertised me as a "big gun" from Michigan. One man in an article in a local paper intimated that, in the words of Artemus Ward, "there might be danger of busting the gun." But this all tended to awaken curiosity, so on our advent we were greeted by large congregations. Sisters Hout and Fleming, together with Sister Anna Kaufman and a younger Sister Hout, and several others whose names I do not now recall, were of great help in the meetings. Mr. Hout and Mr. Fleming, the husbands of the sisters mentioned before, made no profession of religion, and while they would occasionally indulge in a social glass, they were very respectful and always ready to assist their families in getting to the services. A well-to-do and highly respectable family by the name of Mason lived near by. The old gentleman was a class-leader in the Methodist Episcopal church on the hill. He took quite an interest in the meeting at our church. We were invited to their home to dinner one day, when Father Mason told us of his son James, who since his return from the army had become quite reckless, and requested us to talk with him, as he was regular in his attendance at our services. We took occasion to speak to James about the salvation of his soul, and to our surprise he flew into a passion and said he wanted nothing to do with religion. We expressed our surprise and remonstrated with him, when cooling down a little he said, "Of course, real religion is all right, but there is my father; he has been a class-leader for years, and he will ask the blessing at the table and have family worship and get mad before he gets out of the house." We said nothing more to James at that time, but spoke with the old gentleman, giving him the status of the case. The next morning as the family gathered for prayers the old gentleman got out the Bible, but before reading he broke down and asked forgiveness, and they had a new prayer and season of real devotion for once at least. At the service that evening James made his way to the altar and began to earnestly seek the Lord. I presume that James, under the convicting power of the Spirit, was somewhat irritated and undoubtedly a little severe in his judgment of the old gentleman.

On Christmas we had a grand day; the Holy Spirit came in power, but at the evening service we had a little scene not down on the program. Mr. Hout and Mr. Fleming had been down to Mansfield, and having imbibed pretty freely came back in time for evening meeting, both a good deal under the influence of liquor. When an invitation for seekers was given both of these men made their way to the penitent form. All in the house knew the condition they were in, and the entire congregation was as solemn as eternity. Their wives came forward weeping and we gathered for prayer. I went to Mr.

Fleming to talk to him, but he being beyond all self-control cried out, "Oh, I am all right: go and talk to my friend Hout." I went and knelt by Mr. Hout. He seemed to realize his condition, and I said, "Mr. Hout, I am sorry to see you in this condition." He began to weep and said, "Mr. Hart, it is too bad; pray for me." We had a season of prayer, when an opportunity being given to speak, Mr. Fleming jumped up and going to James Mason slapped him on the sholder and cried out, "Hip, hip, Jim, we are going through with flying colors." The service closed with the families of these men in tears and a feeling of regret and solemn awe upon the congregation. At the meeting the next afternoon both men were present and very humbly apologized and asked the prayers of God's people. Allan Haverfield and wife, holiness people, came to us from the Methodist Episcopal church, also a local preacher by the name of Oswald, and we had a strong society, which at different times has been served by the most able men of our conference.

In the early spring I received an urgent request to go to the Huron circuit and attend the funeral of a Brother McFarland, an old man some ninety years of age. His son, Walter McFarland, was a leading layman on that work. This old gentleman was a Scotchman, and for years had been a devoted man of

God. Sister Hart remained to help in the work at
Windsor, while I went north. Brother Bishop, who
was on the Huron work that year, took me with his
conveyance to Plymouth, where the funeral services
were held. It was a warm and very wet spring, and
we had quite an adventurous trip crossing swollen
streams, etc. On our return I concluded to send for
my wife and spend some time in meetings on the
Huron circuit. Sister Hart made the journey with
great difficulty. All around the depot at Toledo the
tracks were under water and trains had to stop some
distance outside the city. At Monroe the bridge
over the Raisin river was gone and passengers and
baggage had to be ferried across the raging ice-
gorged stream. While at the house of Brother
French, in Exeter, I anxiously awaited the arrival of
my wife. Standing one morning by the large, open
fireplace, gazing into brightly blazing fire, in a kind
of a soliloquy I said, "My buggy is at Coldwater, my
horse at Ida, my two children are in Illinois, my wife
in Ohio, and the Lord only knows whether we will
all ever get together again." Brother French, sitting
near by, overheard the remark and was greatly
pleased. But my wife soon reached me in safety,
and in the good providence of God our family were
all finally reunited.

We held some meetings on the Huron circuit and

then went on to Ida, where my horse was, and making a sled of poles, my wife and I started for Coldwater. The snow was melting rapidly, and when on
the second day we reached Brother Stephen Rice's,
near Jonesville, the runners of our pole-sled were so
badly worn we were obliged to abandon that mode
of transportation, so the next morning, putting Sister
Hart on the train, I mounted our faithful horse
"Billy," and made the remaining twenty miles or
more of our journey in safety. We spent some
time with Brother Ellison in meetings in Coldwater.
Our services were held in the court-house. It seemed
to be supposed that these meetings were of the free
and easy sort, and Mormons, Spiritualists and the
discontented generally were ready to air their peculiar views. I soon put a stop to this, however, and
very decidedly gave them to understand that the
meetings were not open to the rag-tag bob-tailed
genus of religionists, but especially for the promotion
of scriptural holiness. This greatly enraged them,
and accosting me as I passed out at the close of the
evening service one of the Spiritualist stripe informed
me that he could see devils all around me as I was
preaching, and that he could see them all around
Mother Pinney (mother of Judge Pinney, late of
Chicago, Illinois). I quietly assured him I could
easily account for that, "for," said I, "John says of

him who would see God as he is, "He purifieth himself even as he is pure." "So," I said, "moral likeness is essential to seeing God, and if you would see devils all that is necessary is to be morally like devils."

Closing our meeting in Coldwater, we decided to go on to Marengo, Illinois. Taking the train at 4 a. m., we went speeding on our way. But the train was altogether too slow for Sister Hart's anxious desire to once more meet her children. She could hardly lean back in the seat, but sitting on the front edge and leaning forward seemed to think she was making more rapid progress. We reached home in due time and found children and friends all well and glad to greet us.

Edson A. Kimball had for several years been a successful business man at Elgin, Illinois. He was a prominent member of the Methodist Episcopal church. Brother Kimball was a special friend of Doctor Redfield. It was through Brother Kimball's influence that the doctor first visited and held meetings in the Methodist Episcopal church at Elgin. Having united with the Free church, Brother Kimball was desirous that a class should be raised up at Elgin. From the session of the conference held at Marengo, September 13-16, 1865, Rev. Cyrus Underwood was sent to Elgin. During the winter a revival service resulted in the organization of a class. Through the means furnished largely by Brother Kimball a fine church was erected. Brother Underwood labored at Elgin until the spring of 1867, when an arrangement was made for Brother Underwood to take my work in Michigan for the summer, and for me to supply Elgin. Brother Underwood labored successfully in Michigan, and at the next session of his conference was sent to Freeport. We went on to Elgin and stopped with Brother Kimball and family while we finished off rooms in a part of the large basement of the church. We finished off two or three rooms and moved in. We commenced street meetings, which, being quite a novelty, attracted a good deal of attention. I would preach at the church at 10:30 a. m., in the street at 6:30 p. m., and at the church again at 7:30 p. m. We had a profitable summer's work. I received an invitation from a Congregationalist minister preaching to a church at a small place about four miles west of Elgin. Several of us went out one Tuesday evening. We had a good, free time, the pastor very heartily endorsing all he heard. On a Sabbath after I exchanged pulpits with this brother. During the latter part of the summer this preacher attended our camp-meeting at Garden Prairie. I remember in preaching one day on the camp-ground he said the only thing

he feared about us as a people was that we would
not be as charitable as we ought, but would be too
harsh in our judgment of others.   The man bid fair
to become a zealous advocate of the doctrine of holiness, but, unfortunately, he fell in with a class of
come-outers and became so embittered and so harsh
we could not tolerate him, and he finally developed
into the character afterwards known as "Stumbling
Stone Johnson." He settled in Toledo, Ohio, started
a paper called the *Stumbling Stone*, and for aught
I know is still dealing out his denunciations against
everybody and everything not just after his way of
thinking.

August 23–28 I attended the session of the Michigan conference, held in connection with a camp-
meeting near Coldwater, Michigan. I was again
elected chairman, and arranging with Brother Underwood to hold my quarterly meeting, returned to fill
out the year at Elgin.

The Illinois conference in the fall of 1867 held its
session at Elgin, commencing on Wednesday, September 18. Our society was not large, but we put a
rough floor into the unused part of the basement, and
getting a large cook-stove and extemporizing tables
we were prepared to entertain a good proportion of
the preachers and delegates at the church.   Mother
Hart and Mother Bishop took charge of the culinary

department, and with other sisters to care for the table we were well equipped. The brethren from the country sent in beef, mutton and vegetables, and we were well provided with eatables. At this session the following brethren were admitted into the traveling connection on trial: W. A. Nobles, W. F. Manley, Lewis Bailey, J. W. Cain, Wm. Neal, Peter Lynch. Joseph McCreery, at his own request, was placed in a local relation. Lewis Bailey had been running a flouring mill at Galva, Illinois, but disentangling himself from the affairs of this life he entered the work of the ministry and became an efficient worker in the cause of God. At the time of his death he was editor and proprietor of the *Free Methodist*. Jonathan Blanchard, president of Wheaton college, came and spoke words of encouragement to the conference. He was especially anxious that the conference should inaugurate a movement in opposition to secret societies. I remember that in speaking to the conference on the subject he said, "Go ahead, boys, and if I can't keep up I will hold on to your coat-tails and look over your shoulder." The conference adopted the following report on the subject:

Owing to the increasing influence of secret societies and the unjustifiable complicity of ministers of the gospel with the same, and believing our position as a church to be in accordance with the word of God in its application to such unhallowed alliances, viz.: "come out from among them," etc., also consistent with the genious of our republican institutions, therefore as a conference we are settled in the sustaining our disciplinary provisions thereon. ⌠And furthermore, believing secret society influence to be a subtle and insidious foe to spirituality, by its substitution of a Christless religion, a system of semi-biblical rites, and a specious charity for the regenerating power of the gospel, we will in all proper ways and by all proper means oppose its blasphemous pretensions, its arrogant assumptions, and its silent influence.⌡ And while we look with pity upon those members of the visible church and ministers of the gospel who affiliate with the same, we regard with righteous indignation, particularly such who actively urge its pretended claims and defend its influence and tendencies, and though as a conference we do not think it wise to adopt any organized movement in special reference to this iniquity, still we think that a concerted action of the various churches of Christ in opposing this evil is desirable, and understanding that such concerted action is to be inaugurated by a convention of Christians in the city of Aurora, Illinois. on the third Wednesday of October, 1867, with the purpose of securing a national convention of Christians who are opposed to this evil; therefore, as a conference we give our warmest sympathy and recommend our people to active co-operation with the same.

The movement spoken of in the report was inaugurated at Aurora, and resulted in the organization of "The Christian Association Opposed to Secret Societies." In the appointments of this year Elgin, Marengo and Clintonville were put together, and N. D. Fanning and Julius Buss were appointed to the work. We returned to our work in Michigan. At this time the Illinois conference numbered 1,085 members with 207 on probation, and the Michigan conference 404 with 249 probationers.

CHAPTER XVII.

MEANWHILE the work was spreading in the Illinois
conference. A Wisconsin district was formed. A
Brother Sumner, living in Minnesota, heard of the
Free church and desired to join. The questions of
the Discipline were sent him, and he answered them
to the Marengo society by mail, and was duly voted
in. J. W. Dake was at that time blocking out a
district in Bureau county.

Brother D. P. Reed, of Galva, a zealous Methodist, heard of one of our camp-meetings, and making
his way to it found it was just what he had been
looking for. He and his wife joined, and a class was
soon organized at Galva and a church built. Sister
Reed some years ago passed triumphantly to the
better land. Brother Reed now lives at Corralitos,
California. He is realizing the fulfilment of the
promises of the last three verses of the ninety-first
Psalm. Brother and Sister Dudman knew the joyful
sound and fell into line. They removed to Chicago,
where for years they stood nobly by the work, their
house ever being a home of rest for weary toilers.
Some years ago Brother Dudman died in holy tri-

umph. Sister Dudman still lives, a pilgrim and a stranger, but filled with zeal and holy joy, as she passes on to that city which hath foundations whose builder and maker is God.

From that part of the work several efficient laborers were raised up. Lewis Bailey, for years a leading preacher in the Illinois conference and at the time of his death proprietor and editor of the *Free Methodist*, Septer Roberts, J. Craig, C. L. Lambertson and others were also raised up and sent out from this part of the work. Brother Travis went over into Iowa and faced the cold winds of the winter and endured the heat of the summer in establishing the work in that state. Conferences known as the Minnesota and North Iowa, the Iowa and others were later organized throughout the West, which further on may be more fully mentioned.

The laborers in the Michigan conference kept on lengthening their cords and strengthening their stakes. Brother and Sister Frink, through Brother Thomas Riley, went down into Richland county, Ohio, and a society which proved to be the germ of the Ohio conference was soon organized. Brother Gitchell struck over into Indiana and raised up circuits and built churches.

The Michigan conference held its third session in connection with a camp-meeting near Coldwater,

Branch county, August 23-28, 1867. I was again elected to the district, having twelve charges. Among the appointments was that of the Coldwater circuit, reading, "W. D. Bishop, and one to be supplied." By recommendation of Brother Roberts an unassuming young man from Livingston county, New York, who had not yet reached his majority, was appointed. Brushing away his tears, he endured the pangs of homesickness, and rising superior to the embarrassment of his native modesty, stood nobly at his post to the close of the year.

At the session of the conference held in the White church, at Raisinville, Monroe county, September 10-15, 1868, a class of five, this young man being one of the number, were received into the conference on trial. With the exception of Halloway Sawyer, who is now in a superanumated relation, B. R. Jones is the only member of the class who is still in the church. Having successfully passed the examinations in the course of study, he was received into the conference and duly ordained both as deacon and elder. In the fall of 1874 elected to the office of chairman, for several years he filled that position with marked ability, and at the session of the general conference held at Chicago, Illinois, in the fall of 1890, he was called to fill the more responsible position of editor of our denominational paper. At the session of the general conference held four years later at Greenville, Illinois, he was elected to the general superintendency. Re-elected at Chicago in 1898, he is now filling his second term in that important position.

About 1868 two responsible men, A. W. Perry and Lyman Parker, with their families, came from western New York and settled at Coopersville, Ottawa county, Michigan. Being staunch Free Methodists, they determined to have our work established in that part of the state. During the fall of that year, by invitation of these brethren, my wife and myself visited their locality and held services at several different points. W. R. Cusick, an ordained deacon of the Genesee conference, had been favorably known by these brethren, and during the year 1869 they prevailed on him to come to their part of the state of Michigan.

I notice on page 401 ot the Life of Roberts, in an article written by Brother Cusick, in speaking of his coming to Michigan he says, "The church was then in its infancy, there not being more than three hundred members in the three states of Michigan, Indiana and Ohio." Brother Cusick could not have had the statistics at hand, as by reference to the minutes of 1869 I find there were reported 807 in full connection and 266 on probation, making a total of 1,073. I speak of this for the reason that the future historian of the church must depend on statements made in the years of its formation, and it is desirable that these statements be as nearly correct as possible.

Brother Cusick had expected to secure the services of Brother Roberts in special meetings at Coopersville, but failing in this, on the advice of Brothers Perry and Parker he sent for me. I reached Coopersville on Thursday and found they had engaged the Congregational church, the only church building in the place, for a four days' meeting. There were perhaps about a dozen out the first evening. On Friday evening there was a fair congregation and a good degree of interest. On Saturday evening the break came when the wife of the leading merchant, the postmaster's wife and several others of the first ladies in town came rushing to the penitent form literally screaming for mercy. On Sabbath the Lord came in power.

Early on Monday morning Brother Cusick went to the leading man of the Congregational church, for at this time they were without a pastor, and laid the case before him, saying to him that the Lord had come and that we did not feel like taking the responsibility of closing the meeting, adding, "but of course if you say so we must stop." Although this man was not noted for any great degree of devotion, he very readily consented to the further use of the house, and we kept on with the services. During the week the meetings increased in interest and power, and before the next Sabbath by a marked providence we had a clear indication of the will of God that meetings should continue. The wife of a blacksmith who had gone to Canada on a visit had suddenly died. This lady was the daughter of a man who had been blessed and who had become deeply interested in the meeting. The husband was not a professor, but husband and father both earnestly requested me to remain and preach the funeral sermon. I did so, and this service made a deep impression on the minds of the people.

The Methodists had no society in the place, but had a few scattering members in the vicinity. Brother Cusick lived about a mile out of the village. I was staying at his house. On the adjoining place not many rods from Brother Cusick's lived an old man and wife by the name of Watson, who were wealthy. Mr. Watson was familiarly known all through that section an "Uncle Tom Watson." These people were zealous in their attachment to the church of their choice. Uncle Tom, with others interested, concluded this would be a good opportunity, by taking advantage of the tidal wave of salvation now coming in, to float their denomination into the chan-

nel of success. They sent to Canada for a man who
had a reputation as a preacher and an organizer.
The man came on and began operations.

Early one morning Brother Cusick went out to
his stable, and, looking over to Uncle Tom Watson's,
saw the old gentleman out in his yard. Seeing him
out at such an early hour, at once Brother Cusick
concluded that something unusual had occurred. In
a few hours Uncle Tom came over to Brother Cusick's,
and with a dejected look and sorrowful tone said his
wife had become insane. Brother Cusick at once
went over, and as he entered the room where Aunt
Rhoda was sitting she cried out in great agitation,
"Oh, I was in Pilate's hall last night and they were
planning to crucify my Savior!" She was in great
agony of soul, but Brother Cusick saw at once that
God had undertaken. Uncle Tom, in his anxiety for
his wife, was glad to have our people visit and pray
for her. Uncle Tom and Aunt Rhoda got grandly
saved and joined our class. So effectually had the
Lord come that all efforts to bring in division and
distraction were completely foiled. The preacher
went back to Canada and our work had a clear field.

I had stayed at Coopersville longer than I had
planned, so returned home. Brother Cusick held on
for one or two weeks, when, it being apparent that
the work had but just begun, at his earnest solicita-

tion I returned. For weeks the work went on in power. Under the labors of Brother Cusick a fine, large church was built. I was called to dedicate it, and Coopersville became the center from which our work spread out through northern Michigan. Brother Cusick and others worked east along the line of the Detroit & Grand Haven railroad. A good society was raised up at Saint Johns and a fine brick church erected. Someone saved here took the fire over into Canada, and this was the beginning of a work which has resulted in the formation of two good, substantial conferences in the Dominion.

Brother James had been appointed to Isabella county, which at that time was considered about the extreme northern limit of civilization. I made one appointment for a quarterly meeting on that work. I went to Saint Johns by cars and took the stage the next day for Saint Louis, whether Brother James met me with his pony and buckboard. Going as far as we could with this mode of transportation we reached our place of entertainment, and then went on foot over a trail to the schoolhouse. This was a new structure and had not yet been chinked up, but, as I told them, there was an intermission of fifteen minutes between the logs. At the close of evening meeting some of the brethren went before, carrying blazing pine torches to light us on the trail. On

Sunday morning a congregation of twenty-five or thirty was out. I inquired of Brother James why the people did not turn out. "Why, bless you." said he, "they are out here from miles around." That section, at that time so sparsely settled, has become one of the finest farming portions of the state, and it has been my privilege in that region in later years to attend camp-meetings of great power.

CHAPTER XVIII.

DURING the summer of 1868 my wife and myself held a grove-meeting in the township of Berlin, Ionia county. W. H. James was preaching on the Isabella circuit at the time and we had quite a number of members scattered through the different counties in that part of the State, which, although it lies far south of the center, was at that time spoken of as North Michigan. All that region, then an almost unbroken wilderness, is now one of the most productive portions of the State. The Free Methodist church had hardly been heard of in Ionia county, but having advertised the meeting in the *Earnest Christian*, as the scattered ones came in from different points singing and shouting and praising the Lord, the people in the vicinity of the grove-meeting were astonished, for judging by the noise they thought certainly there must be a multitude. Brother James and wife and a young Brother Wilcox had come nearly a hundred miles with a horse and buckboard. Some of the people expressed their surprise that so many Free Methodists could be found in that region. "Why," said I, "didn't you know that the north woods are full of them?" A Brother R. D. Howe, a Wesleyan minister and a staunch reformer of long standing, heard the joyful sound, and in the fall of 1870 made his way to the session of the conference held at Holland, Ohio, September 29 and united, taking a superannuated relation; but before the close of the conference year he was called to his everlasting rest.

At this session the conference territory was divided and two districts formed. I was appointed to the Toledo district, having eleven charges, and John Ellison to the Grand Rapids district, having nine charges. I had held a meeting near Concord, Jackson county, where a fine class was raised up, and, under the labors of Brother Jones, another at Eckford, where Brother and Sister Jennings, Brother Mains and others took their stand, also a local preacher from the Genesee conference by the name of John Billings, who, together with his devoted wife, stood nobly by the work.

From the session at Holland Rev. A. V. Leonardson was appointed to Concord and Eckford. I went to that work to hold a quarterly meeting and my attention was called to some old school property at Spring Arbor, which had formerly been owned and operated by the Free Will Baptists; but about twenty years previous to the time of which I write the Free Will Baptists had removed to Hillsdale. The property at Spring Arbor was in a sadly dilapidated condition. There were ten acres of land and two buildings, one of which had formerly been used for a chapel and the other for a boarding hall. The property had been sold to satisfy a mortgage, and aside from a few rooms in the boarding hall in which the preacher, Brother Leonardson, lived, was unoccupied. I presented the matter of a school and spoke of this property at the session of the conference at Holland. The next session of the conference was appointed for the Concord work, but held in the Methodist Episcopal church at Spring Arbor. Brother Roberts was present and presided. Aside from the family of the preacher residing in the old boarding hall I think there was not a Free Methodist family in the township. But it was a rich farming community and the people were hospitable, and I question whether any session of our conference was ever better provided for.

My wife and myself and our baby, which had been born to us at Toledo, Ohio, during the previous year, rode from Jackson, some eight miles, to Spring Arbor, with a Mr. Crouch. I was a little uneasy as to entertainment and inquired of Mr. Crouch what the prospect for caring for the conference was. I suspect he saw I was a little nervous, for he at once replied, "Oh, they are just coming in crowds, everything all filled up; why, by to-night they will be hanging on the fences." You may be assured his report did not tend to allay my uneasiness. But after a little he said: "I don't want to see that baby suffer, so I guess I'll take you folks to my house." I hardly need add that we were royally entertained. Brother Roberts was sent to Brother I. B. Allen's to stop. Just as he was preparing to retire, someone spoke of a Doctor Hanchett living near by. Brother Roberts at once spoke up and said, "Doctor Hanchett—what are his initials?" When told, he exclaimed excitedly, "Why, he was a classmate of mine in college. I must go at once and see him." And late as it was Brother Roberts pulled on his boots and overcoat and started for the home of his old classmate. He was cordially received and the doctor and his wife insisted on having Brother Roberts as their guest during the conference session.

So these men who had when young sat side by side during their college course; after the lapse of years, each as to qualifications competent to stand at the head of their respective professions, unexpectedly meet again. But how differently circumstanced. The one a man of God, strong and robust, destined to years of usefulness and a bright eternity. The other through dissipation a mental and physical wreck and destined in a few months from this meeting to pass into eternity, having made the mistake of a lifetime. On Sabbath morning it was plain to be seen that with Brother Roberts the cross was remarkably heavy. But in the presence of his old college chum he preached a sermon of wonderful spirit and power.

At the session of the conference held at Spring Arbor articles of agreement were presented by the committee on education in which the conference pledged itself, provided the citizens of Spring Arbor would purchase the property at that place and put the buildings in suitable repair, to raise at least $2,000 for the purchase of furniture, etc., "and as much more as shall make the amount thus appropriated equal to the sum appropriated by the citizens." L. T. Frink, E. P. Hart, Charles Mattice, J. T. Gates and D. W. Tinkham were appointed to act in behalf of the conference. The following resolution was also adopted:

"In case the citizens of Spring Arbor do not accept the articles of agreement as heretofore mentioned, C. S. Gitchell and J.W.Vickery shall be added to the above committee, and that said committee be then authorized to take measures to establish a school at some other point."

The citizens of Spring Arbor held a meeting and appointed committees to attend to raising funds for the purchase of the property, but no definite understanding was reached, and conference adjourned leaving the matter open until the session of the following year.

At this session at Spring Arbor, conference voted unanimously in favor of the proposed change in the general rules respecting the use of tobacco. Also with two exceptions a unanimous vote was given in favor of placing the general superintendency under the restrictive rules. The next session was voted to be held at Delta, Ohio. Brother and Sister Frink had commenced meetings at Delta. They procured an old hall which was not considered very safe. At first the Methodists sent an urgent request for them to come into their church. Brother Frink preferred to work where he would be entirely untrammeled, but finally the crowds in attendance being so large as to make it dangerous to occupy the hall, the Methodists supposing that these disturbers in Israel would, for want of a place in which to hold their meetings, be obliged to leave town, withdrew the generous offer of their house.

Thrown out of a place for the meeting, Brother Frink returned to his home at Holland. But the Lord stirred up the hearts of some of the people, and having secured a place they sent for him to come and resume his meeting. Brother Frink was not slow to take advantage of the opening, and for weeks the Spirit of the Lord was poured out and salvation

came. Of course the town was greatly stirred. The
lines were drawn, and the people took sides for and
against. At the beginning of the meeting a local
preacher in the Methodist Episcopal church by the
name of Woods was bitterly opposed to the work,
going so far as to publicly denounce it. The Lord
touched his heart and opened his eyes, and hum-
bling himself in bitter repentance he became one of
the staunchest promoters of the cause. When the
society was formed he united, and stood nobly by to
the day of his death.

Being a good mechanic, Brother Woods helped
greatly in the building of the fine church which was
soon erected. A brother, J. T. Gates, a prominent
business man, became interested in the work and
assisted largely with his means. He gave me a lot.
and selling a small place in Illinois which my wife's
father had given her, we built a house on the lot and
moved to Delta. Brother Frink had arranged for
Brother Roberts to dedicate the church, but for some
reason Brother Roberts could not attend, and the
dedication of the house devolved on me. As the
general superintendent had been expected, it was a
great cross for me to undertake the work. But by
gracious assistance afforded, the indebtedness was
provided for and the house formally consecrated to
the worship of God.

At this time I was acting as chairman on the Toledo and Coldwater districts. John Ellison was chairman of the Grand Rapids, and S. Roberts of the Cincinnati district. We now had twenty-six charges on the four districts, together with thirty-four preachers and over eleven hundred members in full connection. For a time previous to our removing to Delta we lived in Toledo, Ohio. Being desirous of raising up a work in that city, I so arranged my appointments that I might spend some time in meetings there. We secured an old church building down by the river known as "The Old Bethel." It was in an out-of-the-way place and in a bad part of the city. The building was cold and sadly out of repair, but it was the best opening we were able to find, and here we held on for several weeks. No great good was accomplished for our work in the city, but providentially through this meeting the way was opened for our work in the southern part of Michigan.

Living in the township of Madison, Michigan, some thirty miles perhaps northwest of Toledo, was a family by the name of Reed. They were prominent members of the Methodist Episcopal church. LaFayette Reed, one of the brothers, became greatly exercised in spirit over the death and formality which prevailed, and began to earnestly contend for

a better state of things. He became so intensely
wrought up that some feared he was losing his mind.
A strong impression came to him that he must go to
the church and at the next Sabbath morning service
in the name of the Lord denounce their worldliness
and want of spirituality, He felt assured in his own
mind that this would be his final message, and that
immediately at its conclusion he would drop dead.
Firm in this conviction, he sent word to his numer-
ous relatives to be promptly at the church the following Sabbath morning, and arranged for them to
form in procession and follow him to the deliverance
of his final message and to his death. The Sabbath
came, the friends were on hand, the procession
marched in order, the message was solemnly delivered; but there came an important and unexpected
hitch in the program, for Brother Reed did not drop
dead! His good old mother explained matters as
she exclaimed, "Why, LaFayette, it was a death to
sin that was intended!"

Some of the doubters were strengthened in their
opinion as to Brother Reed's sanity, and especially
when, having butchered his hogs and loaded them
into the wagon, instead of taking them at once to
Adrian for market he backed the wagon into the
shed, and, notwithstanding the January thaw, declared he was awaiting orders from the Lord as to

the place where he should take the pork for sale.
Finally, having received satisfactory instruction, he
started with his load of pork for the Toledo market.
His friends considered it hardly safe for him to go
alone, and secured a reliable man to accompany him.
They reached Toledo in good time and sold the pork
at a considerable advance on the Adrian market.

Brother Reed had in some way heard of the Free
Methodists, and further that there were some of that
order in Toledo. So on his arrival in the city he
made diligent inquiry for the sect, but failing to get
any track of them, at about nightfall he left the city
on his homeward journey. Having reached Tre-
mainsville, a suburb out about five miles, he stopped
at the hotel and inquired of the landlord whether he
knew of any Free Methodists. The man at once
replied: "Oh, yes! There are some in Toledo, and
my son-in-law, living just across the street here, is
one of them." Brother Reed quickly made his way
to the house of the son-in-law, Brother Upham, and
was glad to learn that a meeting was in progress in
Toledo and that Brother Upham was attending every
evening. Brother Reed arranged to accompany
Brother Upham to the meeting, and the escort who
had come along to watch Brother Reed, probably
concluding that man who was shrewd enough to get
such a marked advance on the price of his pork

could not be very badly "off" in his mind, readily
consented to return home alone and allow Brother
Reed to attend the meeting and come on later.

At the close of the sermon that evening Brother
Reed, an entire stranger, arose and gave a rather
rambling account of his journey to the city to sell
his "hogs" and of his diligent search for "this people;"
how he providentially came across Brother Upham,
and how his soul was hungering for a better type of
religion. At the close of the service Sister Hart and
I talked with him and invited him to stop for the
night at our house. In conversation with Brother
Reed we learned more particularly as to the condition of his mind and soul. We prayed together, and
arranged for an appointment at a not very distant
date for the schoolhouse in his neighborhood.

In the morning on leaving Brother Reed slipped
a five-dollar bill into my hand, which in our strait-
ened circumstances proved to be of material benefit.
I preached in the neighborhood according to appointment, and this was the beginning of our work
in that section. Sister Reed was a highly intelligent
woman. She fell into line, was a devoted Christian
while she lived, but some years ago passed on to
that land where there is no sin, sickness, storms nor
sorrows, but where reigns endless life and endless
day.

CHAPTER XIX.

THE eighth annual session of the Michigan conference convened at Delta, Ohio, Wednesday, September 25, 1872. Brother Roberts had not arrived and I was elected president pro tem. This was the first time I had been called upon to preside at an annual conference session, and I very keenly realized the responsibility. Rev. L. J. Francisco was elected secretary and Rev. J. A. Wilson assistant. On Friday afternoon Brother Roberts arrived and took the chair. Rev. Lewis Bailey, at that time editor of the *Free Methodist*, was present at this session of the conference. He laughingly remarked as to my expeditious way of transacting the business. I suppose I was quite nervous and perhaps rushed the work through with unseemly haste.

The school question came up again and the committee presented the following report, which was adopted:

"We still feel the need of a school devoted to the promotion of earnest Christianity and sound, solid learning. The effort to establish such a school at Spring Arbor last year was not prosecuted to success owing to various causes. There is still, we understand, a good opening there, and we recommend the appointment of a committee to establish such a school as we need, either there or in any other place which may offer in their judgment superior advantages and inducements. This committee shall consist of the following persons: E. P. Hart, L. J. Francisco, C. S. Gitchell, J. Ellison, Charles Mattice, I. B. Allen, J. T. Gates. This committee shall have full power to establish the school, secure an incorporation and employ teachers, provided they shall proceed no farther nor faster than the means placed at their disposal, or secured by good subscriptions, will warrant, so as not to bring the conference in debt. In case the committee proceed to establish a school we pledge to them our earnest and hearty co-operation."

The same chairmen were re-elected and appointed to the same districts they had traveled the previous year. After the conference adjourned the committee visited Spring Arbor and informed the people there that we were about to establish a school at some point, and wanted an immediate decision as to their acceptance of our offer of the year before. With one or two other members of the committee I went to Leoni, a station just east of Jackson, where the Wesleyan Methodists had formerly conducted a school, and looked over the vacated school property there. When we returned we found the citizens of Spring Arbor in a stir of excitement raising the funds for the purchase of the property at that place. By night their different soliciting committees came in and reported that they had the required amount pledged.

We decided to locate the school at Spring Arbor, signed the articles of agreement, and the property was purchased and deeded to me in trust until an incorporation could be effected and trustees elected. I saw at once that the burden of the enterprise would rest on me, and decided to sell out at Delta and remove to Spring Arbor. Having disposed of our property, I purchased a lot and in the early spring commenced to build at Spring Arbor. In the meeting held by Doctor Redfield at Marengo, Illinois, among the large number saved was one Stephen Ransom, who had removed to Lawrence, Michigan. Knowing him to be a first-class carpenter and a thoroughly religious and reliable man, I at once opened correspondence with him with reference to his coming to Spring Arbor to reconstruct and put the school buildings in suitable repair. Brother Ransom came on and the two buildings, one for chapel and recitation rooms and the other for a boarding hall, were put in condition, and Brothers Roberts and LaDue formally dedicated the property to the Lord in the interest of Christian education.

We had removed to Spring Arbor and rented a house while our house was in process of erection. Needing some lumber, I engaged a man with a team to go to Jackson and haul it for me to Spring Arbor. I went with the man and team to Jackson, where I was to take the train to attend one of my quarterly meetings. Going to the lumber yard, I selected the

lumber, saw it loaded on to the wagon, when the
horses, being frightened by the blowing of the noon
whistle of the planing mill, started to run. Springing
to the head of the off horse I grasped him by the bit
and undertook to stop the team, but they were running with such force that I was dashed into a pile of
stones. My head was badly cut and two wheels of
the heavily-loaded wagon passed over my right leg,
breaking both bones just above the ankle. For a
short time I was unconscious, and when consciousness returned I found myself bolstered up in a chair
in the office of the lumber yard. Looking across the
street I saw a hotel, and told them to take me over
there. A surgeon was summoned, who soon reduced
the fractures and said if I wished to reach Spring
Arbor I had better go at once. A two-seated carriage
was secured, and encased in cushions, with my
broken limb resting on the front seat, I was taken
to my home, where, placed on the bed, I was made as
comfortable as the circumstances would allow.

Before leaving home that morning I told my wife
that I had so many quarterly meetings to hold and
so many camp-meetings to attend, besides looking
after the repairs on the school buildings, that I did
not know how I was to get through with it all; but
before sundown I found myself providentially called
aside to rest awhile.

We had but recently moved into the house we were occupying and were hardly settled, but that morning the children had put up some scripture mottoes on the wall. Lying there on the bed, I began to muse on my condition. My expenses at the hotel and carriage hire had taken all my money but a little loose change in my pocket. I said to my wife, "Here we are, living in a rented house with no fuel and but little provision and I flat on my back with a broken leg." Just then I looked up to the motto on my right and read: "But godliness with contentment is great gain. For we brought nothing into this world, and it is certain we can carry nothing out. And having food and raiment let us be therewith content" (1 Tim. 6: 6, and 7: 8). Then as my mind went back over the work I could think of a good many who would sympathize with me in my affliction and of some who, on account of our radical principles, might rejoice; when, turning my eyes to the wall on the left, I read: "But I say unto you, love your enemies, bless them that curse you, do good to them that hate you, and pray for them which despitefully use you and persecute you" (Matt 5: 43, 44).

Before the day closed an infidel brought a load of wood, and neighbors who, to designate me from other elders who had moved in, already began to speak of me with special emphasis on the definite article as *the* elder, saw that all our needs were supplied.

For three months the Lord very clearly demonstrated that he could carry on the work without my assistance. and further that he could support me and mine just as easily as though I were bustling around loaded down with care and anxiety. Every mail brought remittances, and I told those who came in to see me that I was lying flat on my back and receiving the pay of a congressman.

For several months I was confined to my bed. Money came from parties of whom I had never before heard, one of these being a wealthy coal-dealer living near Pittsburg, Pennsylvania. I afterwards entered into correspondence with him, and the way opened for an extensive revival in the city where this gentleman resided.

Our little house completed, we moved into it, I being carried on a litter. At the dedication of the school buildings, being anxious to attend, four or five of the brethren took me on a lounge to the Sunday dedication service. It was a high day. Rev. B. T. Roberts, Rev. Thomas S. LaDue and Rev. Lewis Bailey were present and took part in the exercises. I paid rather dearly, however, for the pleasure of attending these exercises, for I took a severe cold,

Yours Truly,
Martha Bishop Hart

which brought on neuralgia of the heart, and for a time I stood in the very gates of death. At times the pain became so severe that I could not lie in bed but had to be lifted out into a sitting posture in a chair. By leaning forward in the paroxysms of pain the pressure on my wounded limb turned the sole of my foot completely up to one side. The surgeon had to be called to wrench my foot back into position, which proved to be a painful operation. I became so feeble that the physician could give no hope of my recovery. Sister Hart called mightily on the Lord, and a company of saints, Brother and Sister Gitchell among them, besieged the throne of grace and by prayer and faith prevailed.

One night when I was at the very lowest I had, to me, a remarkable vision. I seemed to be in the eternal world, when all at once I was surrounded by clouds, which formed a vast amphitheater. The clouds were arched above, and below was a deep, dark pit in which demons were raging in boisterous strife. It seemed to me that no power could quell them. Just then I heard the words, "I am the high and holy one who inhabiteth eternity." Looking up to the arched clouds, I saw a bright being whom I at once recognized as the Son of God. As I gazed upon him, with an air of authority he waved his hand and the demons seemed to skulk away in sullen

wrath. The vision so impressed my mind that I
could never after doubt the authority and controlling
power of the Lord Jesus Christ. The next morning
when the doctor came in I told him how wonderfully
the Lord had blessed me and how much better I felt
in soul and body. The dear old man was so affected
he was at a loss to know what to do, but seemed disposed to leave the case in the Lord's hands. From
that time my recovery was quite rapid.

The conference in the fall of 1873 was held at
Saint Johns, Michigan. I was not able to attend, the
only instance in all my work as a Free.Methodist
minister that I have not attended the session of an
annual conference. My father, who had built and
stocked a store at Spring Arbor, was sent as delegate and informed the conference of my critical condition, but that the Lord had wonderfully blessed
me, so the brethren ventured to elect me to the
chairmanship once more.

Judge Gridley, of Jackson, drew up the articles of
association, the incorporation was duly formed and
trustees elected, and we were ready for the selection
of teachers and session of school. I had the general
oversight of the institution, the burden of finances,
securing teachers, etc., all devolving upon me.
Joseph Jones, the well-to-do farmer who greeted
Mrs. Hart and myself so cordially on our first visit

to Michigan, had a family of four or five sons and three daughters. The chief characteristic with most of these was an all-prevailing determination for a higher education. Clark and Frank at the time of our advent were devoting their time to study preparing themselves to enter the state university at Ann Arbor. During our first winter in the state we held a series of evening meetings in the schoolhouse in the Jones' neighborhood. Our afternoon meetings were held in the spacious kitchen of the Jones' residence.

During one afternoon meeting we were startled by a loud knock. Father Jones opened the door, when one of his sons, who was standing there, said excitedly, "A man is lying in the old deserted log house over by the railroad track, and he says this is the ninth day he has been there without food or water, and I have come for help to get him away." Several of the brethren went with him and found the poor man nearly exhausted from cold and hunger. They knew by the snow which had fallen that the man must have been there for at least nine days. Bringing the man over to the house of Brother Jones a bed was prepared for him near the kitchen stove, and we began to administer to his needs. He begged piteously for water. I told him we were giving it to him as we thought he could bear it. Looking up in

my face he said, "Don't you know that three-fourths
of the human system is fluid?   I could take a gallon
of water into my stomach and it would immediately
be diffused through my body and would do me no
harm; give me water."   We gave him nourishment,
and as he gained strength I inquired how he came to
go into the old deserted log house.   He replied, "I
had a school of young men, but the war breaking out
my pupils enlisted and my occupation was gone, and
I started out to tramp through the country.   Walking down the railroad track I became thoroughly
discouraged, and turned into the old log house to
die."   I asked him what his sensations were while
there.   He answered, "For the first few days I was
very hungry, but this passed off, and there came on
an intolerable thirst.   Water was the thought both
in my sleeping and waking dreams.   When awake I
would build air castles, and I thought if I were rich
I would build me a mansion, lay out my grounds,
and in the midst I would have a fountain of pure,
sparkling water bubbling up.   And I thought I would
sit with a cup in my hand and drink, and forever
drink."   I thought how true to nature were the
words of the blessed Master when he said, "Blessed
are they which do hunger and thirst after righteousness, for they shall be filled" (Matt. 5: 6).   First
there comes the hunger, and as this passes off there

comes on an intolerable thirst, expressive of a desire which in its intensity overtops every other desire; then comes the filling.

The poor man's feet were so badly frozen that they had to be partly amputated. This man remained with Brother Jones and became tutor to his two sons, Clark and Frank.

Clark soon entered the university, was graduated with honors, and when Brother Roberts wrote requesting him to act as principal of Chili seminary I wrote Brother Roberts that Brother Jones was only loaned. So when we were ready to open our seminary Brother Jones came on and took charge. As assistants he had Miss Johnson, Miss Davenport, Miss Shepard, with D. S. Arnold as professor of music. Miss Johnson died some years ago in Illinois. Miss Davenport is now Mrs. J. Craig, her husband being a former student of the seminary and for several years a successful traveling preacher. At this writing he is pastor of our church at Kalamazoo, Michigan. Miss Shepard became the wife of a missionary to Bulgaria. They spent several years in the foreign field, but at present I believe are laboring in the Michigan conference of the Methodist Episcopal church.

Brother Jones labored successfully for years as principal of the seminary, but finally gave up the position and turned his attention to farming. After the death of his estimable companion he engaged in teaching in Wisconsin. At this writing he is professor of languages in the Spring Arbor seminary. Brother Arnold spent several years in "The Arnold School of Music," in Chicago, but at this time is a successful professor of music in the Holiness college at Greenville, Texas.

Clark Jones held the position of principal of the school until he saw a a fine three-story brick building erected; then resigned and left the work to others. The seminary has proved a great blessing. Scores of young people in the immediate vicinity have received a liberal education and been fitted for positions of honor and profit who, had it not been for the school, could never have had these advantages. I call to mind a notable case. A lady in San Francisco, California, who with her husband had been a missionary, the husband having died, she had an intense desire to do the best she could for her boys. She wanted to save them from being thrown into the class which on the coast are denominated "hoodlums." Consulting with Rev. W. D. Bishop, of the Seamen's Bethel, he advised her to send them to Spring Arbor, Michigan. The good woman brought them on and placed them in the seminary, at that time under the supervision of Professor Calland. The boys were a little wild at first, but were soon brought to the recognition of proper authority and obedience to wholesome discipline.

We finally removed to Alameda, California. We had entirely lost track of these boys, and for twenty years had heard nothing of them, when one day we saw a very fine painting on exhibition in the window of one of the drug stores of our city. Down in the corner we noticed A. Cederholme as the name of the artist, and upon inquiry learned that this was Adolph Cederholme, a son of the widow mentioned above. As soon as he heard of our whereabouts he gave us a call. He was delighted to recall the experiences of his school days at the seminary. He said he never should cease to be thankful for the principles inculcated, and for the training he received while there. He informed us that he and his brothers had contracted no bad habits, that he was a member of the Presbyterian church, and that his elder brother had died in holy triumph and gone to heaven. He laughed heartily as he recalled the lively meetings and the earnest testimonies of some of the more enthusiastic brethren. One brother would exclaim, "I was born on the field of battle," and another, "I like my spiritual provender warm," and one old brother was ever calling on the Lord for "the 'rale' fire."

Our schools are doing a grand work. These

early impressions are lasting impressions, and these
hallowed influences are moving out in ever-widening
circles for truth and righteousness.

CHAPTER XX.

IN THE early winter of 1873 I had so far recovered from my injuries that I was able to start out once more on district work. We labored for some ten weeks in a meeting at Jackson, Michigan. We used an old Baptist church, At first our congregations were small, and I told my wife I would like to have somebody to preach to, but soon the house became so packed that we hardly knew how to handle the crowds in attendance. During the month of February, 1874, Brother Roberts made us a call and preached several times. (See Life of Roberts, pages 460, 461). In consulting Brother Roberts with reference to the work at Jackson I told him we had several converts, but that they were all poor and we were unable to build a church. "Oh," said Brother Roberts, "it is a good thing that the converts are poor." "How so?" I inquired. "Why." said he, "you will have no rich man to look to and you will be obliged to lean on the Lord; he will open the way." The words proved to be prophetic. The special meetings closed and we organized a society, renting the old Baptist church.

A gentleman of wealth by the name of Wilcox, who had removed from Syracuse, New York, to Jackson, had arranged with one Professor Stratton, an old friend, for an anti-masonic lecture in Jackson. The old gentleman went from church to church in a fruitless search for a place for the lecture. Finally someone told him of the Free Methodist people who worshiped in the old Baptist church. He looked up the pastor, who informed him he was welcome to the house and that he would do all he could to advertise the lecture. At the close of the lecture Mr. Wilcox inquired whether our people owned the house in which they worshiped. When informed that they did not, as he afterwards told us, he said to himself, "By the grace of God and what little means I have these people shall have a house of worship in Jackson;" and ere long not only a nice church but a comfortable parsonage as well was ready for our occupancy.

The conference session in the fall of 1874 was held at Coopersville, Michigan. Brother Terrill was in attendance. He preached a remarkable sermon from the text, "And the armies which were in heaven followed him upon white horses, clothed in fine linen, clean and white" (Rev. 19: 14). He compared the white horses to right principles and the clean linen to right experiences, showing first that we should have a clean, white, personal experience, and second, that we must have Bible issues of righteousness. He warned the preachers against riding nonsensical hobbies. In the love-feast Sunday morning one good brother arose and said, "I thank the Lord I have a good circuit and a clean shirt (personal experience of purity), and a white horse (holy principles) to ride." This session immediately preceded the fourth general conference, which met at Albion, New York. During the session Rev. J. A. Wilson introduced a resolution to this effect: "Resolved, in case the general conference at its coming session sees fit to order the election of two general superintendents that our delegates be instructed to vote for E. P. Hart as the second." I thought but little of this, looking upon it as a matter of compliment on the part of my brethren. I knew that in the east there were older and better qualified men, and had no thought of being elected to that important and responsible position. Having served four consecutive years on the lower district, I was at this session appointed to the Grand Rapids district. B. R. Jones was appointed to the districts I had been traveling. In view of the responsibility Brother Jones was greatly crushed, and for a time it was doubtful whether he would consent to accept the work. But finally the encouraging words and earnest entreaties of his brethren prevailed, and he consented to assume the duties of his new office.

It has been my privilege to be a member of every general conference except the first. This convened at Saint Charles, Illinois, October 8, 1862, and continued its sittings at that place until the 16th, when it adjourned to meet at Buffalo, New York, November 4. It was composed of ten members representing three annual conferences, the Genesee, the Illinois, and the Susquehanna. There being in the minds of the Genesee delegation some doubt as to the legality of the organization of the Susquehanna conference, when the delegates from the Susquehanna conference were by a majority vote admitted to seats, the Genesee delegates withdrew, hence the adjournment to Buffalo. At the adjourned session at Buffalo, as neither of the regular delegates from the Genesee conference was present, the reserve delegates took their seats and the conference went on with the business. At this session the name conventions, for the annual and general meetings of the church, was changed to conferences. Rev. B. T. Roberts was elected general superintendent for the ensuing four years. The general conference finally adjourned on Thursday, the 7th of October.

The second general conference convened at Buffalo, New York, Tuesday, October 10, 1866, where its sittings were continued until Saturday, the 13th, when it adjourned, to meet at Albion, New York, on Monday, October 15, where it continued in session until Thursday, the 18th, the date of its final adjournment. There were in attendance besides the general superintendent eighteen delegates, representing the following annual conferences: The Genesee, Illinois, Susquehanna and Michigan. There being no objection raised, all the delegates took their seats and the business was harmoniously and satisfactorily dispatched. A committee was appointed to apply to the legislature of New York for the incorporation of the Free Methodist church. The committee on superintendency recommended the election of one general superintendent, and Rev. B. T. Roberts was re-elected, receiving seventeen of the eighteen votes cast.

The third general conference met at Aurora, Illinois, on Wednesday, October 12, 1870, and finally adjourned on Thursday, October 21. This session was composed of the general superintendent and twenty-nine delegates from the same conferences represented at the session held four years previous. At this session the general superintendency was placed in the restrictive rules; also the following amendment to the general rules was carried: After the words, "softness and needless self-indulgence,"

on page 31 of the Discipline, add the words,
"especially chewing, snuffing or smoking tobacco for
the gratification of a depraved appetite." These
changes were afterward confirmed by the required
votes of the annual conferences and became the law
of the church.

J. Mackey, a publisher from New York city and
a lay delegate from the Susquehanna conference, at
this session presented a proposition to assume all the
liabilities and indebtedness of the *Free Methodist*
paper, and Rev. Levi Wood, the former proprietor
and editor, signifying his willingness to accept the
offer and the conference pledging unqualified support, the transfer was made, and Joseph Mackey, of
88 White street, New York, became editor and publisher of the church paper. The committee on
superintendency recommended the election of but
one general superintendent, and Rev. B. T. Roberts
was elected. At this session a new conference,
called the Kansas and Missouri conference, was not
only ordered but organized as well. The appointments for said conference were made by the general
superintendent, the general conference ratifying the
appointments. C. H. Lovejoy was made chairman of
the Northern Kansas and Nebraska districts, and
James Mathews chairman of the Southern Kansas
and Saint Louis districts.

The statistics of the church at this time were as follows: Conferences, 5, viz.: Genesee, Illinois, Susquehanna, Michigan and Kansas; number of preachers, 128; number of members, 6556; value of church property, $234,700.

On October 11, 1872, at the Stone schoolhouse near Plymouth, Cerro Gordo county, Iowa, the Minnesota and Northern Iowa conference was organized, Superintendent B. T. Roberts presiding. Rev. T. S. LaDue was elected chairman over the two districts. The number of members was 160; probationers, 47; total, 207.

This made six annual conferences, which were all represented at the fourth session of the general conference, which convened at Albion, New York, October 14, 1874. Brother Roberts and several of the western delegates were detained, and did not reach the seat of conference until the night of Wednesday, the 14th. According to the provisions of the Discipline the conference was to convene at 2 p. m. on Wednesday. Brother Roberts not having arrived, the delegates present were in a quandary as to the proper course to pursue. I advised that we proceed to elect a president pro tem. and a secretary, and adjourn to the following morning. Concluding to follow this advice the conference was called to order, and Rev. E. Owen, a ministerial delegate from the

Susquehanna conference, was elected president pro tem. and I was elected secretary. We then adjourned to meet at 9 a. m. the following morning. When Brother Roberts arrived and learned what had been done he felt greatly grieved. He seemed to think the conference had been organized in order to supplant him. Many of the delegates sympathized with Brother Roberts, and the preacher in charge at Albion being quite outspoken in his declaration that E. P. Hart was responsible for the action taken, some of my friends were disposed to censure me for having taken what they considered a wrong course. I told them I had done what I believed to be right, and could not see how any more suitable action could have been taken. I inquired what course they would advise under such circumstances, and after looking the matter over they concluded the right thing had been done, and at this session the latter part of ¶ 65, page 33, of the present edition of the Discipline, which reads, "But in case no general superintendent be present the general conference shall elect by ballot an elder as president pro tem.," was added.

At this session I was, to my surprise, elected as junior general superintendent. I was surprised because there were so many who by natural and acquired ability were so vastly my superiors. I should have thought that anyone of a dozen or more who were members of that body would have been chosen; but as the vote was declared, if I remember aright, Brother Roberts received the entire vote of the conference and I received 54 out of the 57 votes cast.

At the session of my conference held a few weeks before I had been elected chairman of the Grand Rapids district. Appointing S. Roberts as chairman of the above district, and looking to the Lord for grace and help, I began at once to arrange to enter upon the duties of my new position.

CHAPTER XXI.

PREVIOUS to my election to the superintendency I had attended meetings in Pennsylvania. My introduction into that part of the work was through Brother Clifford Barrett. He was quite a unique character, having for years previous to his conversion been a reckless raftsman on the Allegheny river. With a pack of cards in one pocket and a bottle of whisky in the other, he was ever ready for any wild adventure in which these rough men might engage, but the transforming power of grace had so changed him that with all his natural enthusiasm sanctified he engaged in the work of the Lord with all the earnestness which had characterized his intercourse with the lumbermen of the Allegheny valley. Brother Barrett had attended several of my camp-meetings in Michigan, and was anxious to have me attend some of the meetings in Pennsylvania. He invariably referred to me as "the reformed lawyer," and as quite a number of that class were sadly in need of reformation, when I was advertised for the camp-meeting near Franklin, Pennsylvania, in August, 1873, a general curiosity to see and hear a reformed lawyer was

awakened. On Sunday afternoon I preached from
the words, "For he endured as seeing him who is in-
visible" (He. 11: 27); and on Monday from John
15, 17. I realized special help, and the Lord, to
some degree at least, gave me favor in the eyes of
the people and access to their hearts. Brother B. T.
Roberts was present and preached with great unction and freedom. A young local preacher from the
Allegany district of the Genesee conference was
present, and was held in especial esteem by all who
had the pleasure of forming his acquaintance and
listening to his expositions of the word. At the session immediately following he was received on trial
by the annual conference. He has since become
very generally and favorably known throughout the
denomination, having, I believe, filled about every
position from janitor up to the general superintendency. As chairman of the district Rev. R. W. Hawkins had charge of the meeting, which proved to be
one of great power and success. J. B. Corey, of
Braddock, Pennsylvania, the wealthy coal dealer referred to in a former chapter, was present, and
at his urgent request I arranged to accompany him
home. In the erection of a new school building at
Braddock Brother Corey had induced the directors
to put up an additional story, and this room he had
seated with chairs, providing for the accommodation

of a congregation of six hundred or more. Here I preached one Sabbath, with the promise of a speedy return to hold a series of meetings.

On my arrival home I made provision for my district work, and my wife and myself went to Braddock to engage in a protracted effort. We had large congregations. The hall would be packed to its utmost capacity, with a crowd in the street unable to gain admission. In time of prayer, according to the prevailing custom in that section, everyone would kneel as certainly as they would stand in time of singing. Undoubtedly each posture with the majority was a mere matter of form, but with a congregation of hundreds all kneeling in time of prayer there is at least a show of reverence. Brother Corey had a large number of men working in a coal mine near by. These were punctual in their attendance on the meetings, and many of them were soundly converted. The irrepressible Barrett was on hand and was efficient in prayer, testimony and labor with seekers. In afternoon meetings while the miners were working in the coal shaft Brother Barrett would earnestly call on the Lord to bless the boys in the pit. He would sometimes bound up in meeting and exclaim, "I am going through clickety click with the glory in my soul." As a result of the meeting a large class was organized, and for years the blessing of the Lord attended the work; but finally, through Satanic influence, distraction and division came in and some honest souls were drawn aside. However, by the untiring efforts of Brother Barnhart and a few faithful ones a fine church property has been secured, and the work is in general favor with the people.

On my way to the general conference of 1874, I spent one Sabbath at Braddock and made my way on to Albion, New York, to the general conference session. At the session of the Illinois conference held at Winnebago, Illinois, October 1-6, 1873, Rev. Joseph Travis was elected as delegate to attend the National Christian Convention Opposed to Secret Societies. This convention met in May, 1874, at Cincinnati, Ohio. Among the delegates in attendance was one John M. Rounds and a Doctor Taylor. They were from Summerfield, Noble county, Ohio. They had never before heard of the Free Methodist church, but becoming acquainted with Brother Travis and finding this to be a young and growing denomination, they were extremely anxious that some representative man should visit their place and finally persuaded Brother Travis to accompany them home. He held some meetings at Summerfield and organized a small class. As he was at that time chairman of the Central and the Iowa districts in the Illinois conference, and feeling that his home work demanded

his attention, he referred these people to me and returned to Illinois. So sanguine were they of success
they at once set about building a house of worship.
They kept urging me to pay them a visit, but as my
time was fully occupied I was not able to respond to
their call until the fall of 1874. On my return from
the session of the general conference of that year I
began to plan for a winter campaign. I finally decided to make Braddock, Pennsylvania, my objective
point, but concluded to go by the way of the cities
of Attica, Lawrenceburg and Aurora, Indiana, Cincinnati, Ohio, and then to take in Summerfield on
my way back to Braddock.

Rev. C. S. Gitchell had held a successful meeting
at Attica, which resulted in the formation of a strong
society. He bought a lot, with a large brick house,
which made a fine parsonage. He also built a fine
brick church, at that time one of the best in the denomination.

Mrs. Hart and myself started out on our contemplated tour. Stopping first at Attica, I dedicated
the church, and we continued the meeting, which resulted in the salvation of a number of souls. From
Attica we went on to Lawrenceburg, Indiana, also
visiting Aurora, a town near by. Rev. W. James was
pastor at these points. The work here never seemed
to take very deep root, and I presume hardly a

vestige of it remains, From these places we went on up the river to Cincinnati. Here we found a small class who worshiped in a hall. They were of the extremely radical type, and when persons who were not up to their idea in dress, etc., attended their services, they were sure to denounce them in a harsh, discourteous manner. This they called "Turning the hose on them." As a result they were not troubled with much of an attendance from the outside. I preached one evening here to a small congregation. From the "Life of Roberts" I notice that Brother Roberts in 1872 visited Cincinnati, and although something was accomplished he says, "The prospect here does not look encouraging. I advised them not to continue to rent the church, but to hold prayer-meetings in private houses." (Page 419).

From Cincinnati we went on to Quaker City, Ohio, en route to Summerfield. We reached Quaker City late at night, stopped at a small hotel, and on the following morning took the hack for Summerfield, some fourteen miles to the south. This part of Ohio is quite broken, being diversified by hill and dale and is sometimes spoken of as "the Switzerland of America." We reached Summerfield a little before noon, the hack driving up to a large house standing on the corner. The building had the appearance of a public house, and as we were ushered into the spacious sitting-room we supposed we were stopping at a hotel. Dinner being announced, we were introduced to the family, and learned that we were in the hospitable mansion of J. M. Rounds, one of the men who met Brother Travis at the convention at Cincinnati and by whose invitation Brother Travis had visited Summerfield. Brother Rounds was formerly from Baltimore, Maryland. He was of about average height, but of stout build and quite fleshy. He was a whole-souled man of the truly hospitable southern type. "Aunt Martha," as his wife was generally called, was a noble woman of the domestic kind, who could cook a dinner to the entire satisfaction of the most fastidious palate. They had a family of sons and daughters, of whom but one daughter, Maggie, was at this time living at home, the others having gone out, with families of their own.

We reached Summerfield on Friday. We were warmly welcomed by Brother Rounds, Doctor Taylor and others of the little class organized by Brother Travis. As I have before stated, these dear people were so confident that the Free Methodist church was the one of their choice that they at once erected a nice chapel in which to worship and for the series of meetings which they expected us to hold. So general was the expectation of a revival that even the unsaved were prophesying a remarkable work of grace. Summerfield at this time being some miles from the railroad and not in direct touch with the main lines of travel, and the people through marrying and intermarrying being more or less connected, they were unpretending and simple-hearted. Tobacco-raising was the principal industry. Large tobacco sheds for the curing and storing of the weed were to be seen on every hand.

Doctor Taylor, who was a man of more than average intelligence, was not only the leading physician in all that region, but a local preacher of marked preaching ability. But as a medical practitioner he was without diploma, and as a preacher without ordination. When serving as a private in the war of the rebellion the officers of his regiment, discovering his ability both as a physician and a preacher, decided to have him installed either as surgeon or chaplain to the regiment, but the absence of both diploma and ordination disqualified him for either. They considered him a remarkable but rather strange character. A man of keen perception and a ready speaker, Doctor Taylor was the champion and leading spirit in the anti-secret movement which prevailed throughout all that section. The persons who sympathized with our work at Summerfield from its very beginning were persons who had long stood high in the community.

It was evident that the Spirit was moving on the hearts of the people, and everything seemed favorable for a deep and thorough work of grace. We were announced for Saturday at 11 a. m. and 7 p. m., and for the Sabbath. Our further stay was contingent on the providential indications and the leadings of the Spirit.

CHAPTER XXII.

AT THE time of our advent Summerfield was a quiet little country hamlet, and any incident out of the ordinary was occasion of special remark. So even our coming awakened quite a degree of curiosity and caused a good deal of comment. Soon after our arrival Maggie Rounds called across the yard to a neighbor girl and said, "The new preacher and his wife have come." "Oh," was the response, "have they? Then we shall know what the latest fashions are." Miss Rounds afterwards told us she watched that young lady that Friday evening as Sister Hart in her plain attire entered the church, and on her face saw plainly depicted a look of mingled merriment and surprise. Curiosity drew out a large congregation, and at the very first service the house was crowded. The Lord gave especial help in the presentation of the word, but it was plainly evident that the truth was coming on a line little expected by those by whose invitation we were there.

Professor Blanchard, of Wheaton college, had been at Summerfield and delivered several addresses on secretism, and the expectation seemed to be that our efforts were to be mainly on the same line, so when we began to strike down on deeper fundamental principles even these zealous opponents of Masonry began to feel they had something to do aside from applauding and cheering on this new champion of their cause.

The truth, however, took hold, and from the very outset conviction settled down on the people. By the help of the Spirit I insisted on the necessity of being saved from all sin, and as tobacco-raising, curing and selling was the leading industry and tobacco-using the general practice, I spoke kindly but firmly against these evils. It was evident the plow was going deeper than had been anticipated, and some of our little class began to question the wisdom of coming out so plainly against this Diana of profit and pleasurable gratification. I preached and Sister Hart exhorted, and there began to be a visible melting and endorsement of the truth by outsiders. The main difficulty seemed to be with our own people. They were being reined up to a point of decision where they must take a stand either for or against. It was a crucial test, and poor Brother Rounds on Sabbath evening, as after the service we were seated by the grate in his sitting-room, gazed into the burning embers, and with a long-drawn sigh exclaimed, "Well, we have got ourselves into a pretty boat. I am as empty as a barrel." Doctor Taylor afterwards told us that as he was riding his horse on his round of professional visitation he found himself nervously chewing the weed and vigorously expectorating the juice, and exclaiming, "I wish Hart hadn't come."

On Sabbath I touched a little on secretism, giving some of my own experience, and such a degree of enthusiasm was awakened that the shouts drowned my voice and I had to stop speaking and wait for the excitement to subside. Then as I swung around on to the tobacco, in the oppressive silence I had to stop and quietly remark, "Brethren, it is time to shout." Sister Hart and I talked the matter over, and believing it would be pleasing to the Lord to bring things to a focus finally decided to announce on Sabbath that our stay was contingent on the attitude taken by our people with reference to raising, selling and using tobacco. So at the Sabbath service I gave out that at 11 a. m. the following day we would gather at the church and decide as to the continuance of the meeting. I said to them: "If you will come to the teaching of the word of God as interpreted by our book of Discipline we will gladly remain and assist in the meeting; if not, we shall pack up our baggage and on Tuesday take the early hack for the station."

Now they were in a strait betwixt the two. On

the one hand was the humility and sacrifice involved and on the other was their sense of right and the opinions and speech of the people, for outsiders were already giving endorsement to the truth and prophesying a remarkable revival. We had no fears as to to the outcome, for we were thoroughly convinced that the Holy Spirit was so back of the movement that God's will would prevail and a deep and lasting work of saving grace be realized.

At the Monday morning service I talked on the Discipline, and as plainly as I could set forth our distinctive issues, and finally said, "Now let all who are determined to come to this line gather around this altar and consecrate themselves to God and seek the experience of a clean heart." They all came out and earnestly sought the Lord. At the evening service deep solemnity rested on the congregation, and when the invitation for seekers was given the altar was crowded. From this on I felt perfectly free to preach the whole truth, and the success of the meeting seemed assured.

With each succeeding service the meeting increased in interest. We had preaching at 11 a. m. and 7 p. m. The people were unpretending and simple-hearted, and primitive methods prevailed. From all the country round they would come in crowds, some in sleighs, some on horseback and some afoot.

Women with a child before and one behind and perhaps a baby in arms could be seen astride a horse
making their way to the house of God.   The church
would be crowded at the morning service, and frequently the meeting of the morning would run on
without intermission to the hour for evening preaching.   Sister Hart and I would slip out and get some
refreshments and a little rest, and then go back for a
renewal of the conflict at the evening hour.

Morning and evening the altar would be crowded
with earnest seekers.   As seekers came forward the
brethren and sisters would take the ladies' hats and
extra wraps and hang them on some hooks on the
wall provided for the purpose, for they came forward
with the expectation of wrestling till victory came.
As the penitents knelt at the altar and began to
earnestly cry for mercy the brethren and sisters
would all stand around and lustily sing almost any
hymn or song that might come to mind, but invariably the selection would be one which had no reference whatever to the case of the seekers.   For instance, with an altar filled with struggling, weeping
penitents, the brethren would strike up and at the
top of their voices sing, "Shall we gather at the
river?"   The principal object of the singing seemed
to be to drown the cries of the seekers.   We insisted
strongly on submission and faith, and as we would

strike up and sing some appropriate hymn or song the people for awhile supposed that these were made up by us to meet the demand as the occasion required. As seekers got blessed we had them stand and tell what the Lord had done for them. This was altogether new in the manner of conducting meetings, but seeing such good results the people readily fell in with our methods. Young ladies in the midst of their earnest seeking would rise from their knees and rush to the door to throw away their snuff-boxes, for many of them were snuff-dippers.

Day after day meetings continued from 11 a. m. to 11 p. m., and the slain of the Lord were many. About every night more or less were prostrated under the power of God, who would be taken to their homes in sleighs, to remain unconscious perhaps for the remainder of the night. The footprints of J. B. Finley and men of like stamp were plainly visible all through that region, and there were many who knew how to prevail with God in prayer. Billy Barnes, as he was familiarly called, a man of large, robust frame, and voice almost like a lion, would place his right hand just back of and over his right ear, and in stentorian tones sing with a voice loud enough at least to awaken the spiritually dead. There were elect ladies whose names I cannot now recall who would hold on to God in earnest prayer until victory came. Jennie H., an intelligent young lady, a member of the Methodist Episcopal church, came to a Sabbath afternoon meeting. She was earnestly seeking the experience of holiness, and while I was preaching her faith struck through, and exclaiming, "I have got it! I have got it!" she jumped until her hair fell down her back and snapped almost like a whip. She joined our class, and was afterwards appointed class-leader. She was called, in the providence of God, to pass through the severest tests, but the last I knew of her she was still standing true.

Demonstrations were nothing new in that section. It was customary in the winter to "hold a big meetin', take a shout, and jine church." But this meeting struck deeper, and many got out into clear and lasting experiences. A blacksmith living out about two miles was happily converted. About two weeks after, as on Sabbath morning he listened to a sermon on holiness, he was greatly exercised in spirit and could hardly wait for the sermon to close, so anxious was he to ask about this further work of saving grace. At the close of the service he began to ply me with questions, saying, "Haven't I been converted? Isn't that religion? What more is there?" I replied, "Come to the afternoon meeting, brother, and I will try and make it plain." In the sermon of the afternoon I used this illustration: "Suppose you come to the morning meeting and get blessed, and start home feeling wonderfully well, but when you reach home you find the pigs are in the corn. You undertake to drive them out, but, true to their hog nature, they run in the wrong direction and you chase them around for an hour. How do you feel about it? Of course a justified person will not get mad, but how do you feel about it?" When opportunity was given to speak, the brother arose and said, "I see it; I have this religion till you come to driving the pigs out of the corn." He at once set about seeking the cleansing from inward sin.

The custom in that section had been to open the doors of the church about every night of a meeting, and the brethren were a good deal concerned because I did not give opportunity for the converts to join. I told them the doors of our church were ponderous, and that it required a good deal of effort to get them open. Finally, however, I yielded to their entreaties, and gave opportunity to unite with the class. I do not now remember the number who joined, but at the close of the meeting we had a large society at Summerfield. The class there has passed through severe testings, some have moved away, many have died, and some on one pretext or another have withdrawn, but the candlestick has not been removed, and the things which remain are being strengthened. At different times we held meetings at several points in Noble county. At Freedom, a small place just out from Summerfield, we had a successful meeting. At Mount Tabor I dedicated a church, also one at East Union. These meetings were all characterized by the same spirit of simplicity and zeal which had been so prominent in the meetings at Summerfield. At East Union a frail, consumptive-looking woman came to the penitent form, and after a short but earnest struggle came through into glorious liberty. In perfect time to the lively tune being sung she bounded up one aisle and down the other. In coming down the aisle she made straight for a young man sitting on the penitent form, and sending him heels over head into the altar made for me. Concluding that discretion was the better part of valor, I beat a hasty retreat and took refuge behind the pulpit. An old local preacher seeing my predicament rushed to my aid, and grasping the woman by the hands was for some minutes led a lively dance by the frail but happy sister. Such scenes were of frequent occurrence, and seekers were expected to come out into the light with shouts and manifestations of joy. If any failed in this it was something as Booker Washington recently said about seekers in the meetings of the colored people of the South.

Mr. Washington said: "In the meetings among the colored people of the South if a seeker does not come through shouting and praising the Lord he is looked upon with suspicion and they say of him, 'I reckon he's got the white man's religion.'" One old local preacher at East Union had the reputation of being quite a theologian, and in general he was quite sound, but he could not discern between fore-ordination and foreknowledge, but insisted because God foreknew an event he must have necessarily foreordained it. He failed to see that with a being possessing the attribute of foreknowledge, while it would be impossible for him to foreknow any act of his own without predetermination on his part, he might foreknow an act of another without any personal predetermination.

Several classes were organized in Noble county, and as spring was opening we concluded we would return home, and the prospect at Lawrenceburg and adjacent points in Indiana not being very encouraging, I sent for Brother W. H. James, who was preaching there, and he came on and was duly installed pastor of the work at Summerfield and vicinity. J. W. Headley and wife lived on a farm about three miles from Perryopolis. They had been members of the Methodist Episcopal church for some seven years. Brother Headley held a license as a local

preacher.   This worthy couple were fully up to the
level of their religious surroundings, but knew nothing of the experience of entire sanctification, indeed
had never heard a sermon definitely on the subject.
They had heard of the people called Free Methodists, but what they had heard did not give them a
very exalted opinion of the sect.   A member from
Summerfield went over to Perryopolis and engaged
the church for Brother James for services for a few
days.   Brother James commenced with a Sabbath
service.   Brother Headley and wife were at the meeting, and the sermon on holiness was entirely new to
them and gave them food for reflection.   On Monday morning Brother Headley went to his farm
work, but Sister Headley went to the meeting.   At
night when his wife returned, Brother Headley, being
anxious to know about the meeting, inquired as to the
results and was told that two of their members had
given their names and joined the new class, but as
these were not considered very important members
Brother Headley said, "All right, we can spare a few
more of that kind."   On Tuesday Sister Headley
again attended the meeting, walking three miles
each way.   As she returned at night her husband
found her crying.   He inquired how it went at the
meeting and his wife replied, "Sixteen of our best
members went to-day."   Brother Headley exclaimed,

"Let them go." Sister Headley went on to say, "And these that joined want us to join, too." Pretty thoroughly stirred, Brother Headley replied, "No, I will go to the Campbellites before I will join them." But by Wednesday morning the poor man was so convicted he could not work and concluded he would go to meeting with his wife, and being convinced that the work was right, decided not to be found fighting against God and began earnestly to seek the Lord. The meeting closed with an understanding that Brother James was to have the church to preach in again in three weeks. When at the appointed time Brother James returned he found the church door fastened with double locks. As about four hundred people had gathered, the preacher knelt on the church steps and offered a short prayer, and preaching a short sermon gave invitation to any who might desire to unite, when four more of the old class joined, Sister Headley being of the number. In the fall, at a camp-meeting held near Summerfield, Brother Headley feeling deeply humbled asked to be taken in on probation. Brother Headley was in course of time duly licensed and finally joined the traveling connection, and for several years the name of J. W. Headley has appeared in the conference appointments as district elder.

CHAPTER XXIII.

For the first two years after my election to the superintendency my labors were confined to the West. My first experience in presiding at the eastern conferences was in the fall of 1876. In going to the older part of the work I felt some degree of embarrassment, especially as I had but a partial acquaintance with either the work or the people. For the first time I presided over the Genesee conference at its session held at Parma Center, Monroe county, New York, in the above mentioned year. Here were many ministers who were my seniors in years and vastly my superiors both in natural and acquired ability. Asa Abell was living, and, although feeble, was in attendance at this session. When his name was called and he had given his report some one struck up the song with the chorus,

"O, come, angel band, * * *
Bear me away on your snowy wings,"

when a Methodist Episcopal evangelist by the name of Tinkham cried out: "Don't sing that. I have just come from a conference where a lot of perfumed dude preachers were singing 'Bear me away on your snowy wings,' and it made me sick. Sing for this old veteran, 'Am I a soldier of the cross?'" and the conference joined heartily in singing the war song. This Brother Tinkham was one of the sympathizers with our work in those days of ecclesiastical restraint, but never received the help Joseph McCreery boasted of, "for," said Joseph, "I got so I could run through a troop, and with a little boosting by the regency I went over the wall." At this session also were Henry Hornsby, Levi Wood, John Reddy, S. K. J. Chesbro, William Manning, O. O. Bacon, Ichabod White and others in the itinerancy; and among the laity were such men as George Holmes, Seth Wood-ruff and Velzy and Brainard and Brother Bacon, of Albion, men who had been all through the regency war, and who in the time that tried men's souls had stood true to principles of righteousness. To step in among and preside over such veterans as these, was, for a comparatively young and inexperienced man, standing under a great load of responsibility. But these brethren and all with whom I came in contact were so considerate and so kind that all feeling of embarrassment quickly passed away, and I felt as much at ease and at home as I did among my own brethren, many of whom had been raised up under my own labors in Michigan. This was the last session of conference John Reddy was permitted to attend.

Soon after its close his only daughter was taken with typhoid fever, and earnestly exhorting her father and friends to meet her in heaven, passed triumphantly on to the realms of light and life.

Not long after, the father was taken down with the same dread disease. The only regret he had was that he had not been more zealous in the work of the Lord, and exclaiming to some ministerial brethren standing at his bedside, "We must not only step into every open door, but we must open doors," entered into his eternal reward.

My wife and I went on to the sessions of the Susquehanna and New York conferences, and by invitation of James Mathews and wife spent a day at the great Centennial exposition at Philadelphia. In the summer of 1877 we attended a camp-meeting at Salamanca, New York. Brother R. W. Hawkins was chairman of the Allegany district, and had charge of this meeting. The Metcalfs, from Rushford, and many others of the charter members of the church in that section, were present. A slight veering from the straight line of the established doctrines of the gospel had already begun to be manifest, and my wife and I stood stoutly for the old doctrinal landmarks, and the Lord, greatly to the encouragement of the older members, manifested his approval by copious outpourings of the Holy Spirit. A Brother

Requa was appointed to preach one morning, and as he arose and announced and began to read the hymn commencing with "He dies, the Friend of sinners dies," there was such an unction and spirit attending the reading that the preacher was obliged to stop and open the way for weeping penitents who came flocking to the altar. At this meeting we met a widow lady by the name of Maxon, whose husband had formerly been superintendent of the sanitarium at Dansville, New York. This lady was at this time living at West Randolph, New York. She was quite urgent in requesting us to go to West Randolph and hold a series of meetings in the Baptist church. I finally told her if she would secure the written consent of the trustees of the church allowing us the use and exclusive control of the house we would some time during the coming winter visit the place and hold a meeting. We gave the matter but little further thought, but on our return home from our round of fall conferences we received a letter from the lady enclosing a paper duly signed by the trustees giving consent to the use of the church. Having promised on these conditions to go to Randolph, nothing remained but to make preparations to visit the place, according to agreement. As winter came on we wrote on, giving date of our arrival, and in due course of time found ourselves comfortably

cared for in the home of Mrs. Maxon, and ready to
begin a siege in the Baptist church. It seems that
some years before, when their church was at a low
ebb, this society had secured the services of Evangelist C. D. Brooks, of our Genesee conference,
whose labors had resulted in quite a number of converts and accessions to their organization. I became
convinced that they considered that Free Methodist
preaching was not only as efficient for the upbuilding
of the church as any other, but withal fully as cheap
as to expense, and that these considerations had a
good deal to do with their willing and ready consent
to our use of their house. Seeing this, I determined
that, as far as I was able, the game should be played
for keeps. I had supposed that the society was
without a pastor, but, to my surprise, I found they
had a duly installed shepherd. I have forgotten his
name, but if I remember aright, he was a relative of
Rev. E. E. Adams, who at that time was a member
of our Genesee conference. I found, also, that several Baptist ex-elders belonged to the society. West
Randolph was at this time a rallying point for the
general gatherings of atheists, infidels and free-think-
ers generally. In feeling my way along, to the great
delight of my Baptist brethren, I opened up along
these lines. In this I encountered the opposition of
the infidels, but had the endorsement of the Bap-

tists.   But finally training my guns to a closer range
and doing the best I could to show what Bible religion is and what it does for men and what it causes
men to do, I incurred the displeasure of the Baptists
but received the endorsement of the infidels.   The
Baptist friends were especially chagrined when their
pastor made his way to the altar, declaring he did
not come as a seeker of entire sanctification, but to
be justified, "for," said he, "how can I be justified
when I have failed to declare the whole counsel of
God?"   To add to the discomfiture of the Baptists,
a maiden lady with some means and richly attired,
who was a leading member among them, came to an
afternoon meeting completely stripped for the race;
her gold gone, her high bonnet, built with special
reference to adornment, with dead birds, rags and
roses, entirely denuded, in appearance justifying her
remarks as she rose to testify and said, "I suppose
you think I look as though a hurricane had gone
over me."   The opposition became more and more
decided; one of the ex-elders speaking in meeting
one evening, referring to Sister Hart's happy testimonies, said, "We are not coming here to be
taught by a light-hearted woman."   And now there
began to be talk of closing the church against us.
At this the infidels came to the rescue, declaring, "If
the church is closed we will get the largest hall in

town for you." Miss Ella Hapgood, now Mrs. J. S. McGeary, was teaching school and living at Randolph. She was a member of our church and stood nobly by the work. Among those saved was a frail but interesting young woman. She was a bright convert, but we were about discouraged when we learned she was engaged to a young man who, though upright, was an avowed Universalist, and who belonged to a Universalist family. When we learned of the marriage of this young lady to the young Universalist we gave up all expectation of her making a success of trying to lead a religious life. But judge of our joyful surprise when we learned that, instead of being influenced to give up her religion, she succeeded in bringing her husband and about all the Universalist family not only to her way of thinking, but to her way of living as well. In evidence of this I adduce the fact that F. E. Glass and wife have for several years been filling appointments, first in the Pittsburgh and since the division in the Oil City conference.

CHAPTER XXIV.

ON OUR return trip from Randolph to Michigan, at the earnest solicitation of a committee appointed by some "holiness people" of Oberlin, Ohio, we stopped off at that place and held a series of meetings. Being a college town, and having so many societies and entertainments to take the attention of the people, we concluded we should not get much of a hearing and that our stay would be brief. On our arrival we found that the committee consisted of three brethren, one a colored man, and that they had secured a hall in the third story, in which a society of colored people worshiped. To our surprise, the hall was crowded from the very commencement of the meeting. The color line in Oberlin we found to be very obscure, white and colored people attending the same services, seated side by side throughout the hall. After a few evenings the crowd became so dense that fears for the safety of the building began to be entertained. At the close of an evening service Professor Churchill, one of the faculty of the college, asked me why we did not go to the college chapel. I told him we would be glad to do so if it

could be secured. "O," he replied, "that can easily
be done." The chapel was opened to us, and with
the exception of one or two evenings each week
when needed for some of their exercises, our evening services were held there. Our meeting ran some
three weeks or more, closing up on Sabbath evening
with a service in Finney's church. Mr. Finney had
died a few years previous, and a Dr. Brand was
pastor at this time. Mr. Ronayne visited Oberlin
just before the close of our meeting, and after the
close of our services remained and gave a course of
anti-masonic lectures. (See "Ronayne's Reminiscences," page 419.) Quite a number were saved,
but we did not deem it advisable to attempt to
organize a class. From what I learned of Oberlin
theology I concluded that Mr. Finney, in order to
correct the Calvinistic doctrine of a necessitated will,
leaned to the other extreme, and was finally resolved
into teaching that depravity is located altogether in
the will, and that there is no backlying state or condition of depravity. Consequently to will right is
to be right, so a change of will is a change of heart,
therefore men are bound to change their own hearts.
I learned that Mr. Finney, in preaching on consecration, would single out the chorister, and calling
him by name exclaim, "Do you realize what it means
to lead in the singing of praises to God? Get down on

your knees and consecrate yourself to the Lord." I
was told he would sometimes preach the most searching sermons on bringing the will into submission to
the will of God, but there seemed to be lacking the
one all-essential factor of faith.   Still we found
there some of the most devoted and meekest saints
we have ever met, but these had come to their experience not only by consecration but by faith as well.
Here we met two young students who were twin
brothers; their name I believe was Fuller.   Later
one of them died, and if I mistake not the other has
for years been a missionary in India.   At the close
of our labors at Oberlin we went to our home in
Michigan.   A Brother and Sister Osborne, who were
living at Saint Charles at the time Doctor Redfield
held his meeting there, and who were among the
number of those who came out into the experience
of entire holiness, had removed to Burlington, Iowa,
at which place Brother Osborne with his son was
running a wholesale paper warehouse.   Sister
Osborne had written me repeatedly to visit Burlington and hold a meeting.   I had written Sister
Osborne, making an engagement for the early spring
of 1878.   At the session of the Illinois conference in
the fall of 1877 M. L. Vorhies was sent to Belleville,
Illinois.   Brother Vorhies was one of the finest sing-
ers I ever met.   As Sister Hart was not to accom-

pany me to Burlington, I wrote Brother Vorhies asking him to meet me in Burlington and assist in the meeting. This he readily consented to do. When I reached Burlington I found that Sister Osborne had secured a little brick Baptist church on South Hill. The house was unoccupied, and we had exclusive control. Just before my arrival at Burlington a kind of a tramp preacher had put in an appearance and was quite anxious to begin the meeting, but Sister Osborne informed him that the meeting would not commence until Brother Hart came. The brother went up to clean up the church, and came and reported to Sister Osborne that he had everything in readiness and that he had dusted the organ and placed it in proper position for use. This of course gave him away, "for," said Sister Osborne, "if you were a Free Methodist you would know that they do not use organs in their services." The brother soon left, but he had secured a few days' board, which undoubtedly with him was the main thing. In speaking of the incident afterwards Sister Osborne's son laughingly remarked, "Mother thought she was entertaining an angel unawares." Brother Vorhies arrived in due time and we commenced our meeting. At our first service we had a congregation of perhaps a dozen. Brother Vorhies had a railroad song which he used to sing with telling effect. He

sang that song, and as there were many railroad men
living in the vicinity of the church the song aroused
the most intense interest, and soon the house was
altogether too small to accommodate the crowds
which came out.   A young lady by the name of
Streed, who was teaching in the public schools, was
saved.   She afterwards married Rev. C. H. Loomis,
and for years has borne the burdens and shared in
the victories incident to the itinerancy.   Brother and
Sister Gates were members of the Baptist church
but in these meetings stepped out into the clear
light, and for these intervening years have been
known to our work both in Iowa and Illinois.   An
old lady, a German Catholic, was persuaded by her
little grandson to attend the service one evening,
and went home greatly stirred, declaring that some
one had told the preacher all about her and he had
talked it all out in the meeting, and stoutly affirming
that she would go no more, but the Spirit so worked
on her heart that she came again, was grandly saved
and made a substantial member.   But time and
space will not admit of my mentioning all the sub-
jects of saving grace and the remarkable incidents
in connection with the meeting.   John Burg, so
favorably known among our people, was a member
of the German Methodist church on North Hill.
When the rumor of the meeting reached his ears he

went one evening to the little Baptist church, and being unable on account of the crowd to get inside, stood on the steps and listened to the preaching and the singing, and soon made his way to the fount of cleansing. A good society was organized. Brother Vorhies was duly installed as pastor, and almost a constant revival kept up for a year or more. A fine church building was erected, and in the fall of 1881, as we were on our way to California with our family, we stopped off at Burlington and dedicated the house to the worship of God, Rev. M. L. Vorhies being district elder and Rev. E. E. Hall pastor. In process of time, mainly through the influence of Brother Burg, a society was raised up and a church built on North Hill. The sixth session of the general conference was held in the church on South Hill in the fall of 1882. The winter immediately following, my wife and I went to San Jose, California, to hold a series of meetings. We rented a vacant store-room. I purchased lumber, and with the help of some sympathizers made seats and commenced the work. Brother James Allen and Brothers Kennedy, Clarkson and others gave us encouragement and assisted materially in the meetings. We were entertained at the home of Brother Allen. I paid out my last five dollars for material for seats, etc., and in appealing to Brother Chesbro for funds stated the fact.　Brother Chesbro published an appeal in the paper embodying what I had written, and good Brother John Romine, who was an early convert to our work in Michigan, sent me that amount. The evenings were damp and cold, but we held meetings each evening, first in the street and then in our hall. Ross Taylor, son of Bishop William Taylor, was holding street meetings at the same time in connection with revival services in the Methodist Episcopal church.　We would sometimes join forces in the street, and then give notice of the meetings at the church and in the hall.　One evening a gentleman followed our little band from the street to the hall, who was destined to take quite a prominent part, financially at least, in our work in the California conference.　He was an Englishman.　He took a seat in the back of the hall, but paid strict attention to the preaching.　This man became a regular attendant on our services, but would usually slip out at the close of meeting, so that we did not have much opportunity to converse or get acquainted with him. We had a number of converts, and I gave notice that on a following Sabbath morning I would organize a class.　I occupied the hour of the morning service in explaining our Discipline, and then called for any who desired to unite to present themselves at the altar.　To my surprise, about the first one to come was my English friend. He wore a heavy gold watch-chain, gold studs and a large Masonic emblem in gold.   I judged that the man was laboring under a misapprehension, and concluded he would be ready to retreat when I came to insist on an affirmative answer to the disciplinary questions.   I said to him, "I suppose you wish to join on probation."   He at once replied, "No, I wish to join in full connection.   I am a member of the Congregational church." I called his attention to the questions, especially the ones referring to the wearing of gold and of being connected with secret societies.   He at once answered, "O, that is all right.   Nothing will trouble me but the smoke."   I felt relieved, for I saw the man knew what he was doing, and I quickly replied, "O, the Lord will help you out of that."   The sequel proved my words to be true.   He came out to the evening service with the gold all gone.   He afterwards told me that about three weeks after he united with the church, as he was sitting in his study, Satan suggested that it was foolishness for him to give up smoking, "so," he said, "I took down my pipe for a smoke, but the first whiff made me so sick I could smoke no more."   Then came the suggestion, "Brother Hart told you the Lord would help you out of that, and he has."   When I proposed to the class to send for Brother Vorhies to come from

Missouri to take charge of the work, I inquired what each would give towards his expenses. Brother Brown said, "I don't know that I can ever make a Methodist, I can't talk well enough, but I'll give fifty dollars towards getting the brother out here." The necessary amount was soon provided, and we sent on for Brother Vorhies and family. He labored here successfully until called to his eternal reward. Before his death Brother Brown made provision in his will for ten thousand dollars to be placed in my hands in trust for the work, but after his decease some of the heirs, claiming that the estate was much less than they expected, decided unless I would consent to a smaller amount they would contest the will. To save litigation, and especially out of regard for the widow, I consented to take less than a third of the original amount. This is being used as, in my judgment, I deem best for the advancement of the cause of God. While the growth of the church may not be considered remarkable, it is somewhat remarkable, in view of the stand we take with refer-- ence to profitable and popular sins, that we have been able to maintain an existence. I am satisfied, how- ever, if our records of membership were kept in the loose and careless manner in which the records of most of the denominations are, that instead of being set down at about thirty thousand we should be rated at nearly double that number. I would be pleased to make mention of the noble men and women who in the East and West and North and South have fearlessly taken their stand for truth and righteousness, and who to-day, despite the scorn and contempt of carnal professors and worldlings, are ready at the bugle call of duty to rally around the cross. From personal knowledge of our people I unhesitatingly declare that we have within our pale some of the truest and brightest saints by which the church of God has been graced since the days of the martyrs. May we, by the blessing of God, be enabled to hold inviolate the heritage received from the fathers. Amen!

THE END.

www.ingramcontent.com/pod-product-compliance
Lightning Source LLC
Chambersburg PA
CBHW051820040426

42447CB00006B/298